© Laurie Graham 2024

Laurie Graham has asserted her right under the Copyright Design and Patents Act 1988 to be identified as the author of this work.

All rights reserved.

No part of this book may be reproduced in any form or by any electronic or mechanical means, including information storage and retrieval systems, without written permission from the author, except for the use of brief quotations in a book review.

First printed 2024

Once the sea touches your soul, life on dry land will never be the same again.

Gratitude ........................................................................... 6
What is Cold Water Therapy?........................................... 10
Contraindications .............................................................. 12
Benefits of Cold Water Immersion ................................... 13
How to Start ...................................................................... 15
Breathing Techniques ...................................................... 17
Quick Tips for Dips........................................................... 19
War Wounds and Wisdoms .............................................. 21
Rise.................................................................................... 23
Comfort ............................................................................. 24
The Journey – Its alright once you're in........................... 28
I want to age like sea glass.............................................. 34
Claire Ness, 49, Methil, Fife ............................................. 36
Pauline Gilbert, 45, Grangemouth, Stirlingshire............. 38
Heather Laing, 56, Jackson, South Lanarkshire ............ 41
Kirsty Mcdonald, 47, Leven, Fife ..................................... 43
Jessica Harrison 44 years old, Warwickshire ................ 45
Alison Cranston, 61, Kirkcaldy, Fife ................................ 46
Jenny Favell, 42, West Lothian ....................................... 49
Karen Speed, 42, Kirkcaldy, Fife ..................................... 53
Laura Hall, 47 - Scotland.................................................. 55
Michelle Westaway, 54yrs, St Leonard's, Australia........ 57
A Humble Sea Shell.......................................................... 60
Jenna Lister, 24, Fife........................................................ 61
Paula Baker, 71, Portarlington, Victoria, Australia. ........ 63
Strength............................................................................. 68
Maryanne Jacobs, 42, Edinburgh..................................... 69
Dawn Watson, 54, Livingston, West Lothian ................. 72
Leanne Chlosta, 41, Clydebank, West Dunbartonshire.. 74
Helen Quinn, 57, Newburgh, Fife .................................... 78

June Ewing, 50, Fife .................................................................. 81
Sheila Daly, 70 on my next birthday, Fife. ...................... 84
Female, 36, Kirkcaldy ................................................................ 86
Tamara Harrison, 54, Fife, Scotland ................................ 88
A Huddle of Wildies ................................................................... 92
Dawn Brown, 59, Dundee ...................................................... 93
Karen Thomson, Age 50, Broughty Ferry. ..................... 94
Amy Ritchie (aka Mamma Swan) 44, Lundin Links, Fife. 98
Lorna Green, 50, Central Scotland ................................. 101
Tickle My Toes .......................................................................... 105
Anna Savage 39, Cruden Bay, Aberdeenshire ............. 106
Laurie Gallacher, 51, Dunfermline, Fife ........................ 108
Female, 56, Scotland ............................................................... 110
Jan Buist, 56, Fife Scotland. .............................................. 114
Lesley Henderson, 55, Leven, Fife ................................. 117
Michaela Street, 53, Scotland ............................................. 119
Self Love ....................................................................................... 125
Catrina Kivlin, 63, Perth, Scotland ................................. 126
Lorna Finlay, 64. Fife, Scotland. ...................................... 129
The Light ....................................................................................... 132
Chloe Batchelor, 31, Kirkcaldy, Fife. ................................ 133
Tracy Robb, 53, Leslie, Fife ................................................. 135
Annemarie Munro-Fleming, 43, Inverkeithing, Fife. ....... 139
Harriet Hay, 57, Leven, Fife ................................................. 141
Elaine Hardie, 53, Fife ............................................................ 144
Sandra Berry Gove, 66, Leven. .......................................... 146
Karen Lindley, Nottingham ................................................... 148
Lynne Waddle, 54, West Lothian ...................................... 151
You .................................................................................................. 152
Isabel Traynor, 55, Leslie, Fife, Scotland ...................... 153
Louise Lawson, 56, Dundee ................................................. 154

Sandy Toms-Mann, 37, Hertfordshire ............................ 156
Kreisha Szaranek, 48 years old, Glenrothes, Fife ......... 159
Linda-Lou, 50, Kirkcaldy ................................................. 161
Sarah Griffiths, 49, Cheshire ......................................... 163
Josie McMaster, 51, West Yorkshire .............................. 167
Cristina Wilkie, 54, Perthshire ....................................... 169
Nicky Foulds, 47, Cornwall ............................................ 171
Julia McFall, 52, London. .............................................. 175
By the Light of the Silvery Moon ................................... 178
Understanding Tides and Dangers ............................... 180
Staying Safe .................................................................. 184
Moon Magic and Simple Sea Rituals ............................ 186
Miss Motivation ............................................................. 191
Health, Healing and Happiness .................................... 192
Conscious Living ........................................................... 197
The Wild in the Waves .................................................. 199
Outdoor Swimming Groups ........................................... 200
References and Articles of interest ............................... 203

# Gratitude

Our environment growing up deeply impacts who we are as adults and without even realising, we may adopt many different beliefs from those around us, absorbing other people's opinions and morals which influence our own decisions as we go through life.

Those perspectives of parents, teachers, friends, bosses and anyone else we interact with all help to shape us into an ideal of how they think we should behave in society or at work. However, as we continue to go through our own experiences, we sometimes begin to realise that we might not actually be who they thought we were. We learn to make our own decisions and we grow into someone else allowing our own life experiences through relationships, marriage and parenthood to shape who we are again.

Inevitably for many of us, these often life changing experiences, can cause stress, and darkness can fall upon us while we try to figure out who we are again. This can also be a lonely and confusing time where it may even feel like the whole world is against us. Feelings of loneliness are quite common during menopause specifically or during a period of long-term illnesses like cancer, and for many women this can be devastating to their home and marriage.

The emotional turmoil is often repeated again and again throughout a woman's life journey as all too often, we find ourselves having to adapt our lifestyle to accommodate a growing family.

The thing is, the older we get, the more we see who we want to be as opposed to who they want us to be. We begin to realise that there is so much crap going on in the world and we are not prepared to put up with anymore. We learn to separate ourselves from early life experiences. To be authentic and to let go of it all and just be.

It's so necessary for our wellbeing to be authentic.

So, as you read this book, remember you don't end up anywhere by chance. Arriving at your current destination is completely and utterly based upon the options you were faced with and the decisions you make. YOU get to own your own present moment, each and every day and that really is something amazing! You are your own creator. Even something as simple as reading this book is magical, because you chose to purchase it and open the cover and turn the first page. You brought yourself here, to this very moment, by choice, not chance. Just think about that for a minute.

Now, close your eyes and acknowledge that you are in total control of this very moment. In your own time, open your eyes again. A simple conscious act of closing your eyes and opening them again. Not blinking, but a considered eye closing and "eye opening" function that you chose to do. Yes, I asked you to, but you chose to actually comply. You didn't have to, but you did and it was so easy to do, wasn't it? You were completely conscious in that moment. Totally aware of that simple function. You took ownership of the when and the how. Nobody else did it for you. Just you.

This simple act of mindfulness is frequently underestimated for its ability to calm our overloaded minds and with a little focused attention we can get the peace and calm back. Quite often found in the strangest of ways.

I, like many other women, have found alternative (not so traditional) ways to work through the noise of everyday thoughts to find a little bit of peace, and it doesn't carve hours out of our days or cost a fortune in the process. It's not counselling or psychology and it's not medication in the traditional sense. Instead, it's a community. An incredible community of incredible women who are all finding solace in the sea and sanctuary in the conversations and cups of tea.

These women are reaping the benefits of coming together in oceans, rivers and lochs to experience cold water therapy and in doing so, their minds are more peaceful, their physical health and relationships are improving and the people around them within these groups are building a safe space for the other women they meet along the way. Complete strangers who become more than just swim buddies.

These "swimships" for that short time, whether in the water or over a hot drink and a sugary snack after drying off are foretelling a future of togetherness and unity, without judgement. Without competition. Without comparison.

These women become an incredible network of friends. Of family and acquaintances who are sharing their deep and personal journeys with each other. Some of those journeys are shared in the pages of this book because the women here hope that you will also find your solace in the sea, just like they have.

I want to thank each and every one of those women for their honesty, compassion and authenticity. I am truly grateful and blessed that they have come forward, for the love of "dooking" and the home baking – not to mention the blethers, our common goal for serenity and peace and of course to share our love of the water. We hope by doing so, we can encourage at least 1 other woman to take the plunge for the first time and support them on that journey.

Be prepared, as you read these pages, your own journey is going to unfold into something very special and whether you share your story with others or not, you will most definitely grow along the way. All of a sudden, without even knowing, you will have found yourself again and you won't be able to explain how it happened.

## What is Cold Water Therapy?

Before we embark on our journey over the ocean and rivers and lochs, it's probably a good idea to give a little more information on what cold water therapy is and there is a great amount of science surrounding the benefits of this fast growing in popularity pass time, specifically in terms of happy hormone production.

It's so important to remember though, that it is not just about dunking yourself into a bucket of cold water. Not without the correct support and advice and it's not about jumping in feet first without acclimatising yourself beforehand. It IS about safely entering the water and allowing the cold to penetrate your entire being and to do its magic with your mind.

There are however many benefits and when practiced correctly, these benefits in some cases are life changing.

There is also evidence that supports the claims of cold water immersion triggering the vagal nerve which is responsible for the regulation of internal organ functions, such as digestion, heart rate, and respiratory rate.

For those of you new to Cold Water Therapy or for anyone who doesn't know already, in any water temperature below 21°c can be classed as cold water and, in some cases, temperatures as low as 2°c or 3°c are used for plunge baths and pools. This gives us a great scope for gradually working ourselves to the lower levels after starting off in warmer temperatures.

There are other methods where cold therapy can be implemented, such as cryochambers which use liquid nitrogen and electricity to drop the temperature of the chamber for a short few minutes in an attempt at dropping the body's temperature and kicking in the natural healing process. Either way, you don't need to immerse yourself for any more than 2-5 minutes for your body to benefit. You can obviously stay in longer if you choose to do so, but there are a few things you need to be aware of first.

## Contraindications

There are a number of contraindications that should be considered before plunging yourself into cold water which are listed below. Please, if you're concerned in any way or have some health conditions and are unsure, please, please, please consult a medical professional before going. In the meantime, here's a list of some of the conditions where, if you have any of them, it is not recommended that you immerse yourself into this "extreme sport". Speak to your doctor first

Deep Vein Thrombosis
Peripheral Vascular Disease
Pregnancy (although many pregnant women do participate)
Severe Hypertension
Urinary Tract Infection
Fever
Cold Allergy
Severe Anaemia
Tumour
Raynaud's Syndrome
Uncontrolled Seizures
Pacemaker
Acute or recent myocardial infarction
Chronic Regional Pain Syndrome
Adrenal Fatigue
Vasovagal Syncope

# Benefits of Cold Water Immersion

So, we have mentioned the reasons not to dip in cold water, we should also discuss the reasons why we should do it. Therefore, when you consider the fact that a simple ice pack held on a sprained ankle or soaking your feet in water after a long day climbing hills or trailing the shops can help reduce the swollen feet and ankles, dunking your whole body in the cold water has to be worth a try right, especially if you struggle with pain and inflammation in your body. So many people have reported transformational relief and benefits for the following conditions;

Inflammation
Auto immune issues
Mental health issues
Obesity & type 2 diabetes
Chronic pain
Stress and burnout
Circulatory issues
Menopausal symptoms

You will see from some of the stories here that most of the woman have healed in some way or another, and not just from physical symptoms, but also their mental health and their emotional wellbeing. You will also see that some of these women have found a new version of themselves, without even realising. Most of them had reached a point in their lives that had something missing and not even seeing this themselves until they found it again or until friends, partners, and family members commented on how different they look or behave (for the better).

For the women who have contributed to the pages of this book, it's way more than the "sciency" benefits mentioned in studies. These women (of all ages) share with you something that is more magical and more "spiritual" which is something that isn't really talked about as much. Without realising, out of the blue, the women in these pages are "glowing" inside as well as out. Friends and family comment on how their skin looks healthier and their twinkle is back in their eye. There are so many beautiful, positive changes. I call them the positive side effects of the blethers, the water and the cake and they really are life changing. But don't just take my word for it.

## How to Start

So, whether you do it for fun or with purpose, the first thing you need to do is find a safe place to go. As I mentioned before, this can be in a pod in your garden, a loch, lake, sea or river. Other ways involve the cryochambers in the medical or spa surroundings or even a revamped whisky barrel ice bath. There are even some amazing events taking place and popping up all over the world that are exceptionally well managed on retreats and the likes.

Whichever way you choose to take the plunge, going along to an organised event is probably your first choice and it really is important to reach out to someone who is experienced. Guidance going in is key to your dip being successful and enjoyable. So if you get that right the first time, your journey will be a truly special experience. With the right people supporting you, that little bit of anxiety you might be feeling will soon be realised as excitement.

Focussed and controlled breath work is something that is encouraged and remembering that a little bit of anxiety is a perfectly normal reaction to any "out of the ordinary" situations that are new to you. Trying something new and meeting new people can trigger a little bit of nerves, but this can happen to the best of us. So, when you're ready, reach out to a group or a person within the group. We don't bite, and to quote a fellow floater and good friend "the only thing we do bite are the cakes".

You will at some point, take that step forward and you will get in to the water, but if you do change your mind and decide not to, that is perfectly ok. Nobody in any of the groups will put any pressure on you. It's all on your terms.

You stepping into the water is for you and not for anybody else.

Whoever you decide to dip with, just stay safe. I have added some safety tips into this book for you, but you are always encouraged to do your own research and there are so many great books and online courses available. Other dippers are equally great at sharing what they have learned along the way as well.

Listening to other swimmers and dookers will take you on your very own journey of self-discovery. Raising your awareness of not just the cold water pass time, but through the comforting words and vulnerability of these women, you will find a new way of connecting.

In the meantime, reflect today about where you've been, where you're going and who or what's coming with you.

It starts here remember, and every moment you are breathing is an opportunity to relinquish control and allow the Universe to take you exactly where you need to be.

So, let go and flow as nature intended. Enjoy the scenery along the way.

# Breathing Techniques

There are many different breathing techniques used when doing Cold Water Immersion Therapy and focussed and controlled breath work is actually very useful in various situations where anxiety levels are increased. It's a great idea to research beforehand, but if you're joining an organised event, there will usually be someone who can help guide you in to the water safely. In the meantime, here's a couple of methods for you to help get you started.

Wim Hof Method®

This method is probably the most commonly known as Wim Hof is the iceman after all. Dipping in ice for fun. So, in a seated position, close your eyes and try to clear your mind. Don't worry if you can't do this properly as it's not as important as your breathing. Next, take a deep breath in through your nose or your mouth, then exhale naturally and unforced through your mouth. Fully inhale through to your belly, your chest and then let go unforced.

Repeat this 30 to 40 times in short bursts and after the last exhale, take a final inhale, as deeply as you can. Then let the air out and stop breathing. Hold your breath until you feel the urge to breathe again and then take a big breath in to fill your lungs. When you are at full capacity, hold your breath for around 15 seconds, then let go. That is one full cycle. You need to complete 3 or 4 cycles and after completing the full exercise, take your time to bask in the glory.

Box Breathing

This technique is perhaps the easiest and the most common. Complete 4 cycles of the following.

Breathe in for a count of 4, hold for a count of 4 and breathe out for a count of 4. This can be used in many different stressful situations.

As long as you understand that the cold is going to try and grip hold of your breath and you are able to control that, you will be perfectly fine getting in the water and always lower yourself into the water calmly, on the out breath, never on the in breath.

Remember, everyone experiences the water and cold differently and we don't want to shock the body into fear response or worse. Controlling your mind and body will ensure you have a much more enjoyable experience.

# Quick Tips for Dips

The best tip anyone can ever give you for dipping is to just go for it. Get out there and have fun. The next is to not give a hoot about what everyone else is doing, you will soon realise that it's not a fashion show or a competition. Everyone is there for their own reasons and mostly to just forget about home for a while, but there are also a few really handy tips for you listed below. Take them on board or don't, that's entirely your choice. Either way, I hope they help.

Things you need for your first dip (until you decide you want to keep going)

Tow float (not everyone uses them but it is encouraged when swimming in moving water).
Towel (a hand towel is big enough)
Trainers or water shoes
Swimsuit or shorts and t-shirt
Dry clothes
Something hot to drink for after and a sugary snack

If you're going to continue dipping, your list might grow a little from the above to include some of the following

Mat to stand on when changing
Towelling pullover robe for changing under
Dry robe type coat for putting on once dry (colder months)
A bucket to carry your things to the water
A hot water bottle for colder swims
Camping chair
Snacks
Flask for hot drink

Woolly bobble hat (most groups sell these with logos on)
Fresh water to rinse sand off
A head torch for darker dips
Swim/diving boots and gloves
A wetsuit if you feel the water is way too cold for you (avoid as long as possible)

There is so much more that can be added to this list but they really aren't necessary and definitely not for your first couple of swims.  Make sure this is something you want to keep doing before investing in more expensive items.  There is no point investing in a wetsuit for instance if you decide after your first dip it isn't for you.

Cold water will drain your body's core temperature even after you leave the water, so never stay in longer than your body is telling you.  Always aim to leave the water before your start to shiver and ALWAYS warm up as quick as you can after.

## War Wounds and Wisdoms

Now to get a little more personal.

"Vulnerability is not oversharing, its sharing with people who have earned the right to hear our stories and our experiences". Brené Brown

I never really liked who I was for a long time. Actually, I've not loved myself very much at all most of my life and I've treated myself pretty poorly in the past and for as long as I can remember, not only feeding myself with junk food on a day-to-day basis, but feeding myself lies about not being good enough for pretty much everything. Even when others have said the same, I've allowed myself to listen to them and I believed every word. Taking the punches and adding to the already low self-esteem.

I've broke down into a million pieces over and over again when I've been treated badly, when I should have been fighting back and standing up for myself and I've pushed people away when I should have fought harder for them to stay in my life. My opinions have been tainted by others and I've backed down when I should've stood stronger.

I have messed up more times than I can think about and because I never thought I was worthy of the love from others I've allowed myself to be used.

In spite of it all though, I have succeeded and I have still gone on to be the light that others needed so they could find their way and I did all this while tending to my own wounds, I've continued to pour my love into the world and tended to the wounds of others as well along the way.

I've learned that I don't need to be the people pleaser anymore and I'm learning to love myself again, even after all the mistakes. They have all helped shape me into who I am today and whether you like me or not, I am a WARRIOR. A survivor. A woman scorned, but most definitely a woman warmed.

Not perfect, but definitely BRAVE. Not a pushover, but absolutely UNSTOPPABLE. No longer broken, but instead, MENDED. My cracks shine light for others.

I am me. I may even be you, your wife or daughter, your niece or your sister and if I am, then show them all the mercy they rightfully deserve. Show them your compassion, your love and understanding.

Listen when they speak. Hug them when they cry and if they need to hear it, share with them your own journey. It's never too late to rise.

# Rise

Rise
I'm not perfect by any means.  I mean I have lumpy bits and bumpy lumps.
Wobbly bits and jiggly bumps.
When I look in the mirror, the last thing I see is the woman you see when you look at me.
But I made a decision today to change all that.  And today I decided I'm not that fat.
There's a strong and beautiful woman in me and the deeper I look, the more I can see.
I'm a mother, a wife and a survivor of strife.
A daughter, a sister and God, I have missed her.
Like a phoenix I climb and rise from the ashes.
Changing forever as the wave crashes.
In front of you now and in front of the sea
I'm standing so proud, JUST LOOK AT ME.

LjG

# Comfort

Opening our hearts to each other and sharing stories around fires or coffee tables is something women have done for millennia. We have gathered in circles in nature and in tents, to dance and sing and perform rituals. Its cathartic in the act itself which is so healing for the soul and in many cultures, sharing our vulnerabilities is a sign of strength. Sharing our worries or traumas, is a necessary part of self care and healing through that process is inevitable.

I really do hope you find comfort and confidence on your travels through and over the pages here and a little confidence perhaps, to help you on to the next stage.

So where do I start? Well the beginning is always a good place. At least, that's what I say to others when they ask me that same question, so let's go, here's my journey back into the water.

The first thing you should know about me is that I'm just like you. I don't claim to be something or someone that I'm not. I never have done, and so, I can safely and honestly say that my journey will be very much like the other women here and possibly even you and because of that, I chose to share with you these stories. So you can see for yourself, just how much love we have for the waves and water and how much we want to share that with other women.

As I write this book, I am 48 years old, happily married with 2 grown up girls, one cat and one dog. For work, I run my own Holistic Therapies business and have done for 6 years which I absolutely love. Being able to help others on their healing journey is something I have been passionate about for many years. Since I was a child in fact when I had dreams of becoming a nurse. But I always knew my healing practice was not quite as conventional as the NHS. There was way more to it than that, which is why I now practice healing with energy, crystals, vibrations and sound. It makes perfect sense to me that I should always seek alternatives to Western Medicine. That is not to say there is not a time and a place for those options and I am not dismissing the more scientific approach at all. I do however, always look for the more natural methods which is what brought me to water.

I know this may sound a bit cliché, but I genuinely have always loved the sea and have always been drawn to its shores. Whether swimming in it, listening to the waves crashing against the shore or a sitting beside a little stream watching as it twists and turns over the rocks beneath. It's so soothing and comforting and the ability it has to carve out weird and wonderful shapes in the landscape over years of weathering and wearing down that is just so magical and powerful. Nature truly is an incredible force.

My awe is always in awe when I'm by the sea or rivers and waterfalls. Captivated by the mystery of their history.

Not only do I have an affinity to enjoy the sights, sounds and power of water but I also have so many amazing memories of spending long summer days at the beach with my cousins and for the best part of my early childhood, I spent most of my free time in the water. Lovingly referred to as the "water babies" by my Gran because we were either in the pool, zooming down the flumes, splashing and jumping off the poolside at the deep end with our goggles on. Having the time of our lives and our days "down the beach" started with a quick pit stop in to the newsagents on the way to pick up a bottle of fizzy juice, a giant gob stopper and rice paper for our snacks.

Those were the days where we went out in the morning and only came home for dinner, there were no mobile phones, no internet and no games consoles. So jumping waves, building sand castles for hours on end and playing in the quick sand was our far healthier alternative. I also have incredible memories fishing along the coast with my Dad, collecting seashells, hunting mussels and cockles or crabbing. Even as a teen, when more inland, on our annual trip to "the berries" my step dad would take me and my brother river fishing and I just loved watching the water. Not knowing how much I would miss the stillness and tranquility as an adult while waiting patiently for our catch of the day and it wasn't unusual for us to all pile into cars and head out with the other campers (some of them cousins and others only dubbed the title through generations of meeting up in the same place). Off to the nearest loch for a paddle and a picnic. I smile when I reminisce because there really are so many great memories at the beaches and lochs of Scotland. I am so grateful for these times and looking back now, I never realised just how much I really enjoyed those days together.

The water has always called to me, with love, compassion, joy and so much laughter over the years. I have always intuitively been drawn to spend time in its company and when my life has felt "claustrophobic" or "overwhelming" instinctively, a visit to the beach was what I needed to do to clear my mind.

It makes perfect sense to me now, that being in the water at 630 in the morning, in the middle of winter and in total amazement of the sunrise, is the perfect way for me to recharge my soul. Giving me "a breather" from my often chaotic mind.

I've found a solace in the sea and I hope that by reading the stories from some of the other incredible women whom I have met during my dooking days, that you too find the courage to take your first steps into the water too.

"Into the deep blue sea I go, for no other reason than to lose my mind and find my soul".

# The Journey – It's alright once you're in

My story

How did I end up floating about in the Firth of Forth at "crazy o'clock" in the morning, in the pitch black, in the middle of winter?

Well, I will say that my regular dooking days didn't really start until July 2022, and as I write this page, I'm sitting at around 250 "floats" since that day. However, I have dipped my toe a little before then, New Years Day 2019 being the first dip to trigger my passion. A dip that took place at Kinghorn, Fife, in fancy dress with my mother-in-law in tow and very little equipment.

Off into the water we went with many other crazy folks probably all thinking the same thing "what the hell am I doing?"

The whole experience was so invigorating! Very cold, but definitely invigorating. It was so much fun and it set off a little spark within me. I was absolutely buzzing for days after and made a promise to myself that I would be doing that again.

Fast forward a few months later and I was at it again – a solo dook this time with hubby spotting from the shore while he dug for worms to go fishing. But after those 2 "dooks", I only managed the occasional dip in the sea on warm days. Never considering a proper group swim until the night of the 13th July 2022.

The 2 years leading up to my July swim were crazy. Our country was crazy. My own business had to shut down for months and pretty much the world shut down. It was a very different place to exist in at that time and people were scared to leave their homes.

For me, I delved deep into my own personal development. It became a priority for me to grow during the chaos. I took advantage of our lockdown times at home and moved a lot of my Life Coaching work online. I threw myself in to my own learning, with coaching workshops and self-improvement programmes. The Law of Attraction became a big thing for me and I did a lot of work with Linda Proctor and the late Bob Proctor (Personal Development gurus). I was reading so much on mind-set and manifesting. Authors like Joe Dispenza, Eckhart Tolle and Abraham Hicks were my bedtime buddies. I was thriving on personal growth and meditation was my best friend. I embraced the slower paced life and grew a wider online presence. I enjoyed life at home, but craved the outdoors and nature.

Online healing sessions were created for my clients, and I met up daily for virtual coffee mornings with my fellow therapists. I even hosted online Personal Development networking sessions on a global scale for women struggling with their confidence, self-esteem and self-worth. Their growth, and mine was incredible and we were sharing that with so many more women from all different cultures and communities. Supporting them on their own journey. During this time, I was able to recognise the importance of these "meetings" and how beneficial that "staying connected" was for others. Without that online contact. I doubt I would have managed to get through those long months.

Alongside my online presence, I began walking in nature, taking photos and really just enjoying the healing power of fresh air and mindfulness. My creative interests returned and I found myself drawing again and writing poems (a completely new skill) some of which have been added to this book. My creativity was blossoming and in actual fact, I came out of the lockdown a much more grounded and aware individual. I had "uplevelled" as I like to call it.

Over the months that followed and as people were returning to work full time, I was no longer able to go for the long walks I loved so much. The online events with my friends and colleagues became few and far between and gradually, I was paying less attention to my own self care again and my chronic pain returned with a vengeance. Instead of acting on it though, I just kept pushing on. Ignoring the signs my body was giving me and just kept working hard. I fell back into the same old routines. That is until the 13th July 2022 – a night that changed my life forever.

For a few days before the 13th, a serendipitous post kept appearing on my Facebook promoting an outdoor swim at night in Lower Largo, Fife and myself and my walking buddies (Tracy and Allison) had mentioned how we would like to give it a go. We were drawn to this particular event because it was taking place under the Full Buck Moon and there was to be a huddle around the fire afterwards. It sounded fabulous. The perfect introduction to outdoor swimming.

So, it was agreed that we would go along. We were so excited and got to organising our own little fire to take along with marshmallows for toasting and hot chocolate for afterwards, making sure we had enough for everyone else as well. Little did we know that it would be a night that changed all our lives (for the absolute best) but it would also be that one night that reinforced my own personal love of the sea. I would absolutely fall in love with the ocean all over again.

That night was an incredible experience. We met all met on the beach outside the sailing club in Lower Largo, Fife at the arranged time and were welcomed in with open arms. Meeting strangers on the beach at night was something we were a little anxious about. Like holding a party and hoping people turn up. We weren't sure if we would be welcomed at all or if we would fit in. But none of that was an issue.

The delightfully glamorous Mamma Swan – AKA Amy Ritchie was there to greet us as we arrived and another group who went by the group name "wildskins" had also come along to greet us. They all shared some lovely advice as they explained what we needed to do when we entered the water and made sure we were safe throughout the whole experience. Then, as the sun began to slowly make its way towards the Southern Hemisphere, leaving our skies in the very capable hands of the Silvery Moon, we made our way down to the deep blue sea, and in we went. One step at a time. Into the sea. We splashed. We squealed. We gasped and we let go. We let go of all inhibitions and worries. We let go of anxiety and we totally got lost in the moment.

The sea glistened the most magnificent shades of silky purples and silvery blue hues. The rocks reflected neon colours of orange and pink and the glow on everyone's faces was just magical, as if a dappled piece of art.

That night, the sky met the water and as the two merged, they created the most beautiful sunset painting I had ever seen. Nothing will ever compare to that night, floating side by side with complete strangers in the middle of the sea.

I think we stayed in the water that night for around 45 minutes. Just floating there. Laughing, chatting, singing, bobbing around and squealing with joy. Some of the other swimmers even had twinkly night lights in their tow floats which made them resemble Chinese lanterns. It really was so beautiful and magical to see and be a part of.

When we eventually came out of the water, our hands and feet were numb from the cold, but we had the biggest smiles and they soon warmed up around the fire.

For days after, those smiles never left our faces. Even now looking back, I still smile. That night I walked tentatively into the water with women I had never met before, who had welcomed me and my friends into their group and their community. Women who supported us fully on that journey and I came back out of that water having found a community of incredibly powerful and loving women. I came back out of that water having found myself again. I knew there and then that I would be Dooking for life. It was just the most beautiful experience ever and it was just a matter of time before I would be in again. It was in fact the very next day.

You see, for me, the sea is absolutely the place I feel most at ease. It's a comfort. Even though its freezing, I feel the warmth it holds as it ripples around your body. I feel the cosey hug it offers in its embrace and I feel an incredible sense of belonging. Both in the water and with the people who tag along. The sea is the place where I can just be myself. It doesn't matter what has gone on during the day or the week. In the water, it's all gone and while my days may be filled with stress and pain and baggage, in the water, I am home. Nothing else matters. In the sea, I'm like a star fish and I often just lie back, spread out my arms and legs like and just float with my eyes closed. The jagged edges of the day's interactions softening with the ripple of each soothing wave as it caresses my skin. It's the best feeling ever.

My mind, my body, my aura, all being cleansed and all that heaviness being washed away. The saltiness of the water tending to my wounds, cleansing my soul and clearing my mind. Guiding me home again.

On the wilder days, I am battered around a bit more by those galloping white horses. Those crashing waves. Jumping into them with a determination to not fall over and end up with sand in my suit and up my nose...those days are not so peaceful, but are most definitely welcomed just as much and are absolutely great fun. These wild days are often more needed than the stillness. Just like life, no two days are the same and not every day is perfect.

Each day comes and goes, like the tides and the waves and we just ride them as best we can until we are home again and in the words of Paul Weller "Like pebbles on the beach... like broken stones. They're all trying to get home".

I'd like to say I chose cold water therapy for a reason, but in actual fact, it found me and guided me home again.

# I want to age like sea glass

I want to age like sea glass. Smoothed by tides, not broken.
I want the currents of life to toss me around, shake me up and leave me feeling washed clean.
I want my hard edges to soften as the years pass—made not weak but supple.
I want to ride the waves, go with the flow, feel the impact of the surging tides rolling in and out.
When I am thrown against the shore and caught between the rocks and a hard place,
I want to rest there until I can find the strength to do what is next.
Not stuck—just waiting, pondering, feeling what it feels like to pause.
And when I am ready, I will catch a wave and let it carry me along to the next place that I am supposed to be.
I want to be picked up on occasion by an unsuspected soul and carried along—just for the connection, just for the sake of appreciation and wonder.
And with each encounter, new possibilities of collaboration are presented, and new ideas are born.
I want to age like sea glass so that when people see the old woman I'll become, they'll embrace all that I am.
They'll marvel at my exquisite nature, hold me gently in their hands and be awed by my well-earned patina.
Neither flashy nor dull, just a perfect lustre.
And they'll wonder, if just for a second, what it is exactly I am made of and how I got to this very here and now.
And we'll both feel lucky to be in that perfectly right place at that profoundly right time.
I want to age like sea glass.
I want to enjoy the journey and let my preciousness be, not in spite of the impacts of life, but because of them.

Bernadette Noll

I stumbled upon this poem on Facebook one day and it struck a chord. Although it was a shortened version it was still very thought provoking and I shared it in all the swimming groups I follow. I'm sure it had been shared many times before, but every now and then, it reappears as a beautiful reminder.

It's a loving lament of a woman's journey through life. After doing a little research, I found Bernadette's page and asked her if I could share the poem in my book because it meant so much to so many of us. She agreed, to which I am delighted and honoured.

Thank-you Bernadette for allowing me to share your poem. It's beautiful. Just like the women in these pages. Which brings me nicely to the first story.

# Claire Ness, 49, Methil, Fife

I've lived beside the sea all my life and I work beside it too. We have such a beautiful beach yet I had never been in the water, I always thought it would be too cold etc that was until a friend of mine started up Leven Looney Dookers and that's where it all began...

My life has been a bit different from others, from birth right up until the present day. I was adopted as a baby and always felt as though I never really fitted in and I often felt very lonely inside, something that stayed with me for years even though my Husband and I are celebrating our Silver Wedding Anniversary soon, it was still a different sense of love from what I needed for me, myself. I needed something but didn't know what or where to start. I just knew I needed something to help me through the rollercoaster thoughts going on in my head.

So, because I love the Moon, the Sun and the Stars so much, when I saw my fellow Dookers were organising a Full Moon dook on a cold dark April night, I decided to go along. Boom that was it, I found my happy place, my safe place even if it's 5 minutes that's 5 minutes for me. Being in the water watching the moon rise is the most free feeling ever (I now howl at the moon when I'm in the sea, releasing all built up tension and anxiety does wonders for you)

I've now been Dooking for 2 years and I'm in several Dooking/dipping groups which I absolutely love. If I love it that much why didn't I do it before? I wasn't ready simple as that. I'm a Mum, a Wife, a Daughter but I had never been Claire.

Since Dooking my whole body and health has changed, I've toned muscles I never knew existed. Made such good friends who never judge and are always there for a cuddle, a chat and always a giggle. As for my physical health, well, I was diagnosed with ME last year and my blood pressure was erratic but I now have my blood pressure under control without the use of medication and my ME is not as bad as it used to be. The sea has helped me in more ways than one and I would encourage anyone to give it a go and see how you feel. I've even got 3 body boards now, that I use often and that is so much fun.

Whether it's your first time or your 100th time when start to walk into the water (it can be a bit fresh at times especially when the water level reaches a certain area but it wakes you up) you can feel the smile coming across your face. With your back to the shore, you're leaving that life just for a little while and you're now onto YOU time.

Take the time to appreciate yourself and be grateful for what you have, no matter how tough it is let it go. Clear those thoughts in your head and take a nice deep slow breath. Never think to yourself that you can't do it, because you can do it. We are so used to people telling us what we can and can't do we forget we've got a voice too and it's time to use it.

Tell me a few years ago I would be wild swimming in every weather and every season I would have laughed. Now I'm almost a mermaid xxx

# Pauline Gilbert, 45, Grangemouth, Stirlingshire

I first heard about wild swimming from my ex. It was something that she did on a regular basis, she would advocate that it cleared her head and reset her for the week ahead along with the opportunity to catch up with her pals, so I was eager to try it as I could see the feeling it gave her. On boxing day, we headed up to Ballygalley with her son (7yrs old) and we met one of her pals from the swimming group. I wasn't allowed to go in on boxing day as they said it would be too cold for me (Secretly I was ok with this!!) The Wee man and I stood on the beach (shivering) whilst the 2 of them headed in. The pair of them wandered in with choice words as the sea hit them, you could see it was tough for them, but they got each other through it and 10 minutes later they were out again. They were buzzing when they got out, you could see the euphoria on their faces. At that point though, I was still wondering why they did it!!

For the next few months, I was keen to get in the sea, I wasn't a member of any groups in Scotland and I wanted to try it with my ex before I went out to buy all the gear and joined another group back home.

May 2023 was my first dip at Ballygalley with my ex and her son who also loves a dip. It was a chilly afternoon the waves were choppy. The wee man had no fear, so I think that encouraged me to go in without showing any hesitation. It was like nothing I have encountered before. So many emotions, the fear of the unknown when you are in there, the feeling you get when the waves hit you, you forget everything else that is going on in your life so you can fully embrace the moment. The 3 of us had the best time and it is a memory that will stay with me forever.

I will always be grateful to my ex for getting me in the water, and I got to share my first experience with her and her son which was just perfect. I had my second dip in June, again at Ballygalley with my ex and her pals from her swimming group, this was a totally different experience it was a roasting hot day the sea was calm, and it was about 7pm in the evening. We all had such good craic and floated about in the water for what seemed like hours just chatting about anything and everything.

I finally got it. I understood what my ex meant when she tried to explain the feeling of being in the water the buzz you get.

I knew I couldn't just do this when I was NI so I was keen to find groups near me in Scotland so I could dip more often. I scrolled through FB to see what options were near me and found that Fife had lots of options, I went out and bought all the gear confident that this was something that I had a peaked interest in, so I joined a few groups over in the Fife area and on Saturday 8th July, I joined the fife floaters at Seafield for my very first Scottish dip. I was so nervous as I had never met any of the people before and I am socially awkward and not great in big groups. I had no idea what their set up was.

On the day, I pulled on my big girl pants and headed over. Everyone was so welcoming and chatty, although I had dipped before everyone made sure that I was alright when I was in the sea. I could tell straight away that this was a group that I was going to like. I went back on the Sunday to some of the same people from the day before and some new faces, again everyone was lovely, and the craic was mighty. I was buzzing, I had just dipped in the sea 2 days back-to-back.

The time you are in the water for me is a time to forget about all the stuff that is going on in my head a time to reflect on the previous week, reset for the week ahead and be thankful for what we have on our doorstep. The chatting after the dip with a coffee and a wee cake just tops off the dip for me. I do not get to dip as often as I would like due to work but I do get over to Fife most weekends.
I have seen a shift change in my mental health since joining the Fife Floaters I was not in a good place when my relationship ended. My job is lonely I am on the road mon-fri most weeks but knowing that I can dip at the weekend gets me through the week. Without Fife Floaters I am not sure where I would be today. I can't recommend this group enough they are so welcoming and are helping me through some trauma – they don't know this I just appear happy cheery Pauline ready to dip and banter. I have only been dipping with them a few months, 16 dips to date and every single one of them has benefitted me whether it has just been the social side or the getting in the water and forgetting everything.

If you are thinking about dipping just do it!! I can tell you some of my story as to why I decided to dip but it's hard to articulate how good it is!

# Heather Laing, 56, Jackson, South Lanarkshire

On 6th May 2023, I got in to a pretty cold Irish Sea to record a video message. 9 magnificent gal pals all over the world did the same. We ended up with 10 video clips made in or beside the water in Mexico City, Islamabad, Montenegro, Cyprus, Europe and the UK – that were turned into a declaration of love and support for our open water swimming mad friend, Angela, who was battling cancer. Only some of us knew our brave, feisty, funny, intellectually brilliant friend was dying. The message she sent in response to ours was joyous. I replied by WhatsApp:
"It is a tiny gesture of love, my friend. I hold you in my heart and – having braved the Irish Sea – think I might try a bit of open water swimming. When I do, I will think of you always. I hope your days are filled with love. Hx".

On 3rd June, my incredible friend passed away peacefully at home surrounded by her family.

I feel like wild swimming was a gift to me from Angela. As one of the organisers of a planned memorial swim for her – and remembering what I'd said about swimming – I thought I'd best make sure I could participate. In the 3 months since I made that decision, I've gone from literally dipping my toe in the water to swimming with my great friend and swim buddy, Eileen, in our wonderful Scottish Lochs, the Firth of Clyde and the Irish Sea. I've also travelled to Hove to swim in the English Channel with Angela's wife Tonya. She made me cry that day when she told me about scattering some of Angela's ashes at a favourite swim spot in Cornwall and watching her sparkle in the sun as she drifted off.

Thanks to Angela I've found a wonderful new community, added camping (as a first timer) to my journey and also tried paddle boarding (I'm very bad but willing to learn). I've found peace, joy and challenge in the water. I've also found a way to stay connected to my wonderful friend who was a massive influence, gone too soon and missed always.
One of Angela's final messages to me – she couldn't speak toward the end of her time, so I have this great collection of messages – was this: "I think when you go anywhere and see the sea or just something that shows you the possibilities of life then raise a glass and assume I am not too far away".

You are never far from my thoughts and always in my heart, Angela Perfect. You gave me so much love, laughter, wisdom, gin and just joy. And you gave me swimming. Sending you waves of love, my friend and gratitude for this most special of gifts.

# Kirsty Mcdonald, 47, Leven, Fife

My name is Kirsty, I'm 47 years old. I moved to Leven in August 2021 to be closer to my parents as I had problem with drink and drugs (I was an addict).
Not only was I an addict, but I suffered for many years with anxiety, depression and also mental health.

I was asked by my cousin Vicky who stays nearby to go for a dook one day and at first I was like "in the sea? No chance". However, I went with it. I thought "why not just try it once?" so I did and I did it another few times after! When I read up about the benefits of cold water therapy, I decided to look into joining groups in the area and found the Fife Floaters, Fife Dippers, Leven Looney Dookers and the Dookin' Dragons. I found many more and joined them all and just watched for a while.

I took the big step, probably July 2022 when I went for another dook with a group. I took my mum along too and it was amazing. We felt welcome by everyone and were shown the correct way to embrace the cold. That feeling while I was in the water was amazing-my head stopped going at a hundred miles an hour-my head was actually empty for the first time in I don't know how many years.

I felt peace, calm and refreshed. The full day after that dook was amazing too. I thought to myself "I'm going to do this again" and I did and went a couple of times a week with the all the groups in Leven. Then, in February 2023 I finally felt strong enough to get the right help with my addiction problems as well. I realised I couldn't do it on my own, and Dooking then became a major part of my recovery too.

I go out every day in the water (when safe) and sometimes double dook. It has helped so much with my anxiety and depression and now when I notice my mood spiralling, I know a dook will make me feel so much better.

I have met loads of amazing people and the support I have got from them all is truly amazing. I say to so many people, "if you haven't tried it, just do it. You have nothing to lose". It's definitely been a Godsend for me. I've gone from racing head to clear and free and to reset.

Love Kirsty

## Jessica Harrison 44 years old, Warwickshire

I first heard about wild swimming back in 2020/21, The Wim Hoff craze. I was training at the time with Michael Bijker to become a breath work instructor and it was breath work that led me to where I am now.

Around the same time I went into an early Menopause, I was early 40s and after a year of suffering with mood swings and flushes I was also starting to see the middle age spread creep up on me, so I decided to take the plunge into the cold waters.
Straight away I found that it made me feel alive, invigorated and with my knowledge from the breath work training I was doing, it helped me self regulate my own nervous system.
I've been doing Cold Water Immersion, (mainly swimming but also cold Ice baths) for 2 years now and I haven't looked back.

My training and personal experiences as well as my passion has led me to become a Retreat Facilitator with Transformational Breath work and Cold Water Immersion, so I'm a huge ambassador for diving into the deep cold waters to heal and I just love to help others who are suffering with trauma, anxiety and depression. I know first hand, through Cold Water Immersion and with the right breathing techniques that we can break down conditioning and behavioral patterns from my past in mind body and soul.

Anyone that is thinking whether to take the plunge or not, then trust me when I say it will change your life, it has for me personally & professionally the health benefits out way the fear. Take the plunge.

# Alison Cranston, 61, Kirkcaldy, Fife

My dipping journeys.

I had always been a swimmer, being brought up in North Berwick my summers were spent either on the beach or in the open-air swimming pool. We didn't have a name for this kind of swimming and it was not "wild" or "cold water", just enjoying being in the water with a mother who made sure I was home for teatime.

Years of summer holiday swimming in the Mediterranean followed, but over the last few years other than holiday swimming, and the occasional swimming pool visit, I thought that opportunities to take the plunge in our own waters had disappeared. I was left gazing longingly at the sea from our Fife coastline and could only dream of getting in.

As I got older though, I did get more "feart" and phrases like "it's too cold to swim in the Forth" were often echoed by others, so, I put it to the back of my mind and just got on with life.

As time went on, I began to see through social media and chatting with friends that there were groups of folks who had faced their fear and done it anyway. These people had taken the plunge into our beautiful waters and were loving it, but still there was a reluctance from me and with phrases like "am I too old" "am I too fat?" "Is it too cold?" and "what will I wear?" my own fear magnified. More so, because there was no way I was getting into a wetsuit! Also, I was so concerned about what the other dippers would be like, would they be welcoming, would they be young slim, athletic swimmers in wetsuits?

So, I hit the age of 60 and just decided to really research how I can get into the water. After a few months I found Fife Floaters via social media and had my first "dip" on the 14th of August 2023. I had no "equipment" but a swimsuit, a towel and big cardigan. The Fife Floaters could not have been more welcoming. A spare float was brought along for me, another person gave me her water thermal socks and I was looked after so well by the group.

Stepping into the sea was not as cold as I had imagined it would be with the coordinator watching me and reminding me to take it slowly and breathe easily, I walked into the sea and gently lowered myself into the cold water. Feeling the cold water, smelling the salty air, and watching the sky warm up made for a wonderful first experience. The coordinator made sure that for my first time that it should be short, and so I got out and immediately felt the cold. Getting dressed after that first dip was more of a challenge than dipping in the sea.

Since that first dip I have managed to get out once or twice a week. Every single time it has been a "new" experience. For me it's not just about the actual physical dipping but the sounds, the smells the sights, I have witnessed some amazing sunrises which I would have never seen if I hadn't joined the Floaters. I have also found the relationships made with other dippers, the acceptance of everyone, the comradery, the laughs, the chats in the water and the looking out for each other. I really feel I have made some lovely new friends.

Physically I find that any "aches and pains" just disappear while I am in the water, I get a "fizzy" feeling throughout my body that lasts for hours and the energy I get is fantastic, getting up early means I am much more productive for the rest of the day.

Mentally, emotionally I feel dipping in the water being close to nature connecting with the beauty around us has settled me, it has such a calming effect, and it gives me joy. Looking at the photos that have been taken you can see that is clear.

I would say that if you have been thinking about doing this, then give it a try, challenge yourself because once you have, you will feel you can do anything. Some friends have said "oh you're brave!!" It's not being brave, it's just doing something for you, something that you know is doing you good and it makes you feel alive and connected to this beautiful world. Someone said it's not being in the water that is difficult, but getting in. But isn't that the same for a lot of choices in life, it's that first step you have to take that can open up a whole new world filled with new experiences and possibilities and getting into the water has done that for me.

## Jenny Favell, 42, West Lothian

Hello! I am Jenny, I'm 42 years young and I live with my husband, two daughters and Miniature Schnauzer in West Lothian, Scotland. The past few years have been tough and so we rewind to the Summer of 2020. We were all adjusting to some normality once again after the pandemic and constant restrictions of lockdowns. Home schooling and trying to support my daughters' mental health had an impact on my own wellbeing – but I didn't know it, yet. My work life had just changed too as I'd been asked to look after finance and accounts, something that was new to me, but my methodical organised brain hinted that I would be good at it; and enjoy it.

August came along and we rejoiced in companionship, retreating to a cabin in Glen Affric with my parents. I will never forget our visit to Plodda Falls where it became gravely apparent my Mum had been feeling unwell. Thinking it was general unfitness due to pandemic restrictions she hadn't really told us how ill she felt. Within a week of our return, she had undergone surgery and 2 days later given life changing news. Terminal cancer. I did what a lot of people do. Threw myself in to everything and kept going. 'I'm fine, I must look after everyone else. Juggle the home/family life, go to work, support Mum, it's all fine, just keep going…'

Christmas break. We all stop, and I realise I AM NOT OK. From this point on I experienced one almighty burnout. I felt completely broken, beyond repair. My brain was in utter overdrive, and I could barely function. I was stuck in fight or flight mode. The first few weeks were the hardest. Unable to eat, sleep and of course completely unable to look after anyone else. My husband was my rock and slowly helped me piece things together – understand what was happening and why.

It took me months to fully understand what was happening to me, and why. Reflecting on all the stress that occurred via lockdowns, the new role at work (which I didn't enjoy!) and the massive emotional turmoil. As I tried to get back on my feet, my brother introduced me to the water. Ludicrous. I had never been outdoorsy (very much the black sheep of the family!)
So off we went to Loch Clunie - all suited and booted in borrowed wetsuits. A few minutes after I got into that water it struck me. Literally hit me. The brain chatter and anxiety had stopped. It had to stop as I focused on what I was doing. It was a massive relief, just for a few minutes.

That's where my journey began. I had found the magic of cold water. I realised there might just be a way out - a means of control. I was curious about this 'magic' and began to read books and research the benefits of cold water therapy. It provided me with hope and filled me with passion.

For me, at that time, joining a community group was daunting. It felt intimidating and I just didn't have the confidence to go along to a mass event. Then one day I spotted a post from a lady and her friend saying they were going, and anyone was welcome to join. That felt more comfortable, do-able. I went. And again the following week with the same lady and a few others joined. I found my tribe and the most amazing group of friends that I now honorably refer to as Swim Sisters. We shared our journeys to water and developed a love of adventuring. Even if we were unable to get out for a swim, we were making lists and planning day trips.

By August I had resigned from my job and returned to education. Having been a lecturer in FE for many years previously, it wasn't an option to return to that level of stress so instead I work freelance, delivering learning and development sessions online, with a focus on well-being and mental health.

Fast-forward to the present day and not only am I a qualified Cold Water Therapist, I have my own business swim guiding and introducing others to outdoor swimming. I continue to study in the field of mental health, stress management and resilience. It's been almost 3 years now of wild swimming and I have hundreds of swims and dips under my belt. I swim all over Scotland from the emerald waters of Glencoe to the crystal-clear pools of the Cairngorms.

My business now funds a good cause project which provides free sessions for anyone who may benefit from cold water therapy but has barriers to accessing it. I'm trying my best to reach as many people as possible and share the benefits of cold water therapy & outdoor swimming. I focus on offering small group, safe introductory sessions. For me the benefits have been endless but experience is showing me that everyone gains something from it.

As well as the benefits to my physical, emotional and mental health, I have gained friends, adventure and joy from my love of blue spaces. I have become more knowledgeable of the science which supports the benefits of cold water therapy & outdoor swimming. It has been my saviour through the process of losing my beloved Mum… and it has been my teacher.

If you're looking for inspiration, follow my travels on Instagram The Cold Water Therapist (@where_there_is_water) • Instagram photos and videos See what my business is doing on Facebook and here on my website The Cold Water Therapist | wild swimming Scotland | Scotland, UK

# Karen Speed, 42, Kirkcaldy, Fife

Around summer of 2019 I was out for a nice walk along Burntisland beach and decided to have a paddle in the water, it was crystal clear and looked so inviting. The feeling of the cold water splashing over my feet felt fabulous. The next thing I know I was up to my chest in the sea, and off I went swimming through the calmness of the cold sea. I had a huge smile on my face and giggled away to myself as my husband looked on from the beach shaking his head and shouting "you're off your head". I didn't even have a swimming costume on, just my short and T-shirt. I even had to drive home wrapped in the blanket from the car.

From that day on I was and still am addicted to sea swimming. Every bit of spare time I had I found myself down at the beach, sometimes swimming 2 or even 3 times in one day. But why? What made me crave being in the cold, salty water so much?

I suffer with fibromyalgia and I started to notice the more I swam I had less muscle soreness, it really reduced my body pain and the inflammation. I had less fibro flares, it was amazing and I just felt pure buzzing after each dip. I even started to notice my stress levels, anxiety and my low moods start to lift. It was like as soon as my body was emerged into the cold water I was being healed and my body would release endorphins. I felt more alert and my energy levels increased. Family and friends started to comment on my skin, saying it looked lovely and glowing and I would smile a huge cheesy grin and say " oooo that's the sea water".

In lockdown I noticed more and more people starting to take to swimming in the sea and I started to meet others when I was out and about. Other groups were starting to form with swimmers and I joined the Bonnie Black Swans, Seafield Sinkers and also Fife Floaters. I met up with them for arranged swims, it was such a great sense of community spirit and I just felt so connected with everyone and really enjoyed being around others who also enjoyed the experience of being in the sea.

Some amazing friendships have been made, all walking into the sea with our tow floats swinging by our legs and wearing our braw woolly hats. Some of us maybe feeling stressed, anxious or maybe a wee bit down as we go in, but as soon as those waves hit us, then you would see those smiles appear on everyone's faces, hearing the giggles and laughter (maybe after a few little swear words and a wee moan that "it's bloody baltic") but each one of us would leave with a huge smile on our faces.

Wild swimming is a huge part of my life now and it helps balance out my hormones and all my troubles seem to wash away when I'm in the water. It's the best thing I have done and I'm so thankful to be able to appreciate the wonders of the beautiful oceans we have around us.

I think everyone should be prescribed some "vitamin sea" it will truly fill your heart with so much joy and happiness.

# Laura Hall, 47 - Scotland

I've always loved swimming and the beach is my happy place. I've swum in the sea since I was tiny and I've just never really stopped.

In my 20s I lived in the Midlands and I really missed being near the sea. I had a good group of friends I'd go on weekend camping trips with. We'd always stay near a beach and go swimming and bodyboarding together. I think that's the point when I began to get a real mental health boost from sea swimming. I knew it was good for me, so I would seek out opportunities to go. We had a saying "You never regret a sea swim!".

In my early 30s I moved to a seaside town and then I could swim in the sea whenever I wanted. There was a friendly and welcoming swimming community and even a beach hut for sea swimmers to get changed and make a cuppa - luxury! That's when sea swimming became a regular part of my week all year round. I remember one chilly day in that time between Christmas and New Year going down to the beach on my own, stripping down to my cossie and going in for a dip while a big family out for a festive dog walk looked on in horror with their mouths open. It was hilarious!

Now I'm in my 40s and I feel really lucky to be living on the Fife coast with so many fantastic swimming spots in easy reach. Plus I'm now part of a huge family of friendly swimming "clans" and everyone looks out for each other. I especially love going out for a morning swim and being in the water with the gang at sunrise when the sea turns gold – it's magic.

I've met loads of wonderful people and made some good friends through swimming but the main thing I love about it is all the adventures I've had. I've swum through Durdle Door in Dorset, I've been coasteering, I've swum under waterfalls on a hike in Bannau Brycheiniog, swum in stunning Scottish lochs, been out in big Atlantic rolling waves in Ireland and dipped in tidal pools in Cornwall. I've got plenty more locations on my wish list to look forward to.

These days everyone thinks you need loads of expensive kit to get started, but you really don't need anything special. Just wear your cossie, add a t-shirt if you want to be more covered up, and an old pair of trainers to protect your feet and to give you a bit of extra confidence. Always go with a friend and you'll be grand. Don't overthink it, just do it!

# Michelle Westaway, 54yrs, St Leonard's, Australia

Hi, I'm Michelle, I live in a small town on the Bellarine Peninsula right on the bay. I started cold water swimming on the 9 march 2022. A friend and I were swimming all that summer after we did Pilates. Then one day she told me there was a group called the Salty Bitches and suggested we should join them. She went on to say that the time they swum was 6am and I thought no way. Getting out of bed at 8am us too early for me.

My friend went along anyway and then told me how wonderful it was. So, through a total fear of missing out, the next day I went and that was it, I was hooked. I knew straight away that I had found my tribe and I felt fantastic afterwards. My cold water swimming journey started and I was there every day, Monday to Friday at first.

As it got colder I thought I better get a wet suit but I didn't end up wearing it and I just put a wet suit cap on instead, with my bathers. Yes it was cold but it felt bloody amazing. I tingled all over and my skin went a fantastic red, making me feel alive.

I have been swimming for 19 months now and I swim every day, unless I go away on a trip. The longest time I have swum in a row is 98 days straight. My husband always tells people "Don't get her talking about swimming as she will talk for hours" but home has also said the change in me is amazing. I was always a bubbly person but he said it has also grounded me more. I've noticed also how great my skin looks and I just feel great in general. When I skip a day

I miss it so much, like I have lost something. It's not just the water I'm missing though, it's the community we form too. As a group we help each other. We are each other's shoulder to cry on or to laugh with.

If you feel alone, down or just need to find your tribe, try cold water swimming find a group you feel comfortable with and just take that first step you will not look back.

The group I'm with have organised shop tours. I hire a bus and where ever we are going we shop and lunch. There is a lot of laughing and talking and they all look forward to our days off. It's just another way to do things together. So please go let the sea set you free.

Michelle x

"When you encourage others, you in the process are being encouraged because you are making a commitment to that person's life. Encouragement really does make a difference". Zig Ziglar

# A Humble Sea Shell

A Humble Sea Shell

A sea shell holds a thousand secrets
She's full of worries and woes
From mermaid murmurs and water sprite wishes
And Nymphs and Nixie sorrows
There's the Sailor shanty and their wondrous dreams
Of beyond the harbour wall
On a journey, they will carry you
If you listen to their call
Far over all the oceans
And off to unknown rocky caves
The wind will catch their scalloped edges
And drift you straight across the waves
On to a world of magical wonder
A place you feel in your soul
Just close your eyes and let her share with you
The secrets that she holds.

LjG

# Jenna Lister, 24, Fife.

I started properly dipping this year. It was at a time I didn't realize how much I needed it in my life and how much it would become a massive part of me. Not only for my physical health but my mental health too.

I have suffered with painful hips for the last 4 years and I had to give up so much through it. I haven't been able to go on long walks like before and had to change job roles to make things easier on me. It also made my mental health hit rock bottom.

The dips have helped me to get fitter and feel normal again. Being able to do the same things as everyone else and having fun whilst doing it with amazing people of all ages. I have felt my hips get stronger and pushed myself to take part in as many dips as possible.

In February I lost my best friend of 18 years through cancer, I completely lost myself in grief. I was a shell of the person I used to be, not knowing what to do without my person who had always been there. The day he died I went down to Aberdour beach and just stared at the sea. For some reason being near the water made me feel at peace, it was the only place I wanted to be. Chloe kept encouraging me to come for a dip so I finally went along. It was like an instant load taken off my shoulders, I felt free.

I continued to go on the weekly dips and was soon hooked. It has helped me get back to being my true bubbly self, chatting to people I have sometimes never met before but feeling like I have known them forever. My stress levels from work have decreased and it has given me something to look forward to again.

I lost so much in my life so quickly and I never could have imagined that I would ever begin to feel happy or like myself again. The swimming community is nothing like I have come across before, everyone is so friendly, encouraging and always there for each other. I have not only found a better version of myself but a place I feel I belong.

The views and water have the best way to relax you. Nothing can compare to the waves crashing off of your body and the cold working its way through you awakening your senses. With each wave that makes its way back to sea you can feel the tension and stress leaving your body. The feeling after a dip is nothing I have ever experienced before, I feel free. Free to be the person I want to be and a happier healthier version of myself I never thought I'd find again.

# Paula Baker, 71, Portarlington, Victoria, Australia.

Since April 2022, I've been doing a diary entry for each day that I swim with my beloved "Salty Bitches" ……. and sometimes there's a couple of "Numb Nuts" who join in. Here is my first entry, which is pretty self-explanatory, and I can't believe that I've just ticked over 300 swims since that day.

"Fri 22 April 2022: Day 1 Portarlington Pier. Very 1st Swim with the Salty Bitches, after reading an article in the Port Report, I decided to go and give it a go…………..0630 at Portarlington Pier, absolutely the most perfect conditions, warmer in the water. Teeth chattered on the drive home, hot shower, hands still cold sometime afterward, but felt great."

The "Port Report" mentioned above is the local newsletter for Portarlington, it's a seaside town on the shores of Corio Bay, which is on the Bellarine Peninsula in Victoria Australia. The article I saw just explained who and what the group was, and if you fancied joining in to "have a swim, have a water-walk and chat, or just generally 'bob-about', then come and join us. You don't have to be a 'swimmer extraordinaire', you don't have to swim kms, you don't have to compete". Perfect!!
I vividly remember that day as being one that I battled with my inner voices, because for most of my life I've been terrified of deep water, having almost drowned as a child in a school pool, aiming to complete my 'swimming skills certificate' of all things – dog paddle didn't cut it and I sunk rapidly to the bottom of the pool, unnoticed by any adults, there happened to be a vigilant classmate who managed to

pull me to the surface to safety – even though he's no longer with us, thank you Michael Sparks. And there my journey with the Salties began.

I remember vividly, that first morning, watching the folk walking along the Pier on the way to catch the ferry across the bay to Melbourne, and I'm wondering to myself what the hell I was doing, in the water, wading in, getting deeper, it was cold, I was cold, plenty of shrieking, lots of laughing, chattering too, voices and teeth!! But it was exhilarating!! I knew no-one, but we were all together, like-minded women, in the water, sharing the moment. Introductions made, names forgotten immediately, until the next time, I made that my mission – remember names for next time. I love to document events and remember dates, so why not remember swims – if I was to do another one that is!!

How good it is to look back on all the days that have passed and review the conditions, the participants each time, the swim venue, a special thing that might have happened on any particular day/night. Because not only have I managed to swim at the break of dawn, or sometimes mid-day or afternoon during the summer, there have also been numerous 'nudie' swims, to honour particular lunar events on the calendar through the year – recent Harvest Moon swims have been very special, with perfect conditions and wonderful après swim celebrating, with mulled wine and sherry (to ward off the cold of course) and sweet goodies which are always another draw card.

In March this year, I underwent a hip replacement procedure, I swam right up until a week beforehand, to prepare myself for what was to come, knowing full well that mobility would be an issue. My 'tribe' then gathered themselves around me, providing meals, bringing coffee, loading me into a car to take me to my local beach to sit in the sun, and taking my dog out for his exercise.

I couldn't have asked for a more concerned and caring group of women, some of whom have worked in the medical industry, so it made me sit up and take notice when advice was given, I certainly didn't get away with much that's for sure.  5 weeks post-op and I was back in the water again, doing what I love most, the movement I achieved was astounding, after hobbling across the sand with a walking stick in hand, the moment I hit the water, I forgot about how I'd struggled.  There's been a few in the Salties group that've had various surgeries and have maintained that the recovery time was so much better, accrediting the water, the movement and most of all, the support of such a positive 'tribe'.

Now……… here's another thing that's happened since I became a 'Salty Bitch', ideas get 'floated around' (pardon the pun) while we're out in the bay, and it amazes me just how many great 'splinter groups' have been created from casual conversations………..i.e. the weekly Salty Stitchers, who get together to knit and crochet at our local coffee spot once a week.  There's now a cycle group, no competition, just great companionship, who ride to a coffee stop and ride home again.  And the wonderful Op shopping jaunts that have taken us and the lucky Op Shop venues, all by storm.  More often than not, each outing has a theme, there's one planned for November, to find a 'posh frock' to wear in the water on Oaks Day, (Ladies Day on the Melbourne Cup Racing Calendar), this year, we're designing and making our own 'fascinators'!!

While there's been plenty of frivolity, there's also some great serious business going on too. Some of the Salties have recently completed an 8-week initiative for those over 60 to retrain and retain basic core strength and fitness. Put together by a local bowling club, with funding from Bowls Australia and the City of Greater Geelong, one of our Salties members made sure those who were interested were given the opportunity to be involved.

This will also contribute to the next step some Salties are considering – there's a local annual ocean swim event in February, known as the 'Wreck to Reef' swim, with a selection of distances to be swum, and some will swim as competitors. But there are some Salties who would like to 'have a go' but just need that little bit of extra technique tweaking to make it easier for those who may be just stepping out of our comfort zone.

The Salties 'squad training' is going to begin early October, our first couple of days will be spent onshore – perfecting our breathing techniques, so we will be able to conserve energy, this will be very informative, this is just so exciting to be a part of, and I'm really looking forward to being able to make the challenge of distance swimming easier.

As I finish this little essay, already on our Salties Facebook page there's an itinerary up for the next Op shop outing – a lunch stop included. The "Salties on Wheels" are discussing the next ride on the 21st October. And the first Friday of every month celebrates all those who have a birthday during that particular month, with a table full of goodies and hot drinks, which due to the partnership we have formed with a local yacht club, has enabled us to make a permanent base in their clubrooms, and share the great kitchen and bathroom amenities. We've been included in the club's newsletters, with invitations to enroll into their Learn to Sail classes beginning soon, hoping that we can become regulars on the water too.

I'm pleased to have had this opportunity to spread the word about 'wild swimming', although most of our swimming is pretty calm, it's the Bitches that are 'wild'!!

The companionship of such a diverse group of women, who are willing to give anything a go, and create any kind of opportunity to extend their experiences is something I am so grateful to have become a part of. It's changed my life.

**Strength**

"She was strong, but not because she went through so much. She was strong because she carried on. Her fear was not enough to hold her back and her determination was stronger"

LjG

# Maryanne Jacobs, 42, Edinburgh.

My story from the present to the past and how water is my therapy.

Today water (particularly the cold wild Scottish waters) serves my body well. My name is Maryanne Jacobs, my a 42 yr old women, mother, sister, daughter, partner, carer & lover of life! I'm based in west Edinburgh! But I float over to East Lothian too! I have a caravan there and enjoy escaping the city! My life is full in all the good ways! Yet sometimes the beaches on the east call to me!

I live at present with many health conditions & chronic pain, I choose plant medicine & cold water for my medicine & healing. Rheumatoid arthritis & fibromyalgia & Gilbert's syndrome are some of the diagnoses from "medical professionals". I like to trust and believe in my body and only use western meds when very necessary as my body is very sensitive.

Nothing numbs my pain like cold water. I feel alive both in the water and pain free. It reduces my inflammation levels for me to carry on week to week. I not only support my own well-being at present with water, but I also lead a women's recovery dip & connection group where we dip, connect, move, dance & be together. This is a Glasgow based charity called recovery rhythms
https://www.facebook.com/RecoveryRhythmsGlasgow

We call ourselves "the moonlight mermaids".
We dip & dance (optional of course) on the beach in Edinburgh every Wednesday at 7pm in Portobello. The

space provides an alcohol & drug free connection for women 18+. Some mermaids join for the fire & connection but not everyone swims. Recovery is for everyone and I'm also a mentor for Simplify and Create, supporting families in creating deeper connection.
https://www.facebook.com/simplifyandcreatecoaching

My first cold dip was on a cold New Year's Day with snow on the sand and many fires around. I went from wearing a wet suit to skinny dipping pretty quickly. When you have a body that doesn't work as well as it used to you learn ways to make life more comfortable & wearing as little as possible in the water & dancing around a fire to dry off became the best therapy I've found.

I think my first very COLD dip might have been around 4 years back. Maybe 2018 as I've always enjoyed swimming so I've naturally encouraged others to do the same, my children included.

Being a mum, as I home educated both my children, we spent many years outdoors as outdoor education was where our days felt peaceful! My children often inspired me to jump in the sea or wild waters so summer dips and swims were joyful & good for our souls! We always felt connected being outdoors together. We felt connected to nature & community. It's been the root of our well-being.

I spent a summer at gladhouse reservoir inspiring other families to get into the water & supported them throughout and have started a group called family wellbeing & walking community on Facebook where we would camp, walk, swim, dip and play in nature together. This group still exists but it's been a while since we have dipped, we have continued to meet for local gatherings & litter picks. **https://facebook.com/groups/647170175886765/** We would learn together in the community, building fires, eating, cooking, dipping & connecting with nature & being together with many families. We would do herb walks & learn about the seasons together with consistent meet ups. I would never dip alone, or advise anyone too. I not only support others but feel it's important to feel supported too. Nature is powerful and we should respect that.

I would highly recommend anyone looking for connection, well-being, clarity & mental and physical wellness to get into the water! Find a free group or community where you can unite and share your journey.

Our ancestors would be proud to see us walking back home to the ways of nature. In a busy world, a full & sometimes crazy & heavy feeling life… know you can choose to slow down, take a dip & enjoy the presence while you are alive. With gratitude & breath. Let's walk back home. Together.

## Dawn Watson, 54, Livingston, West Lothian

A chance scroll on Facebook in March 2020 and I was intrigued by a post from 'WanderWoman' who was hosting a 'Bonfire & Swim' to celebrate International Womans Day in Portobello. The post drew me in and after 'clicking' I was attending. Shortly after clicking the button, a couple of friends and an acquaintance at the time contacted me, they too were keen to go so we all travelled together, unsure of what to expect.

This day 8th March 2020 is forever in my heart! Crowds of woman were on the beach, bonfires were lit and squeals of joy were heard, probably for miles. Other than dipping my toes in the sea I had never actually swam properly in the sea and as a nervous swimmer I was anxious and slightly terrified at the thought of going in in 'skins' – I don't think I even can remember swimming in the sea as a child! As well as the sea dip making me feel alive and screaming with joy, I have continued my wild swimming journey with my sea loving friends….my soul sisters Claire and Ali.

I remember that day having my breath taken away when I managed to get my shoulders in the sea. Gasping but feeling totally exhilarated at the same time. I remember laughing, giggling, and feeling truly fantastic, which lasted for ages and when I got home I couldn't stop telling anyone and everyone about my sea dip!

Looking back, it was THE best thing to have happened to me and at the perfect time as not long after we were all in LOCKDOWN during the Covid Pandemic. Not to be deterred I squashed all my blue bin rubbish into one bin and cleaned the other out ready to be used as a makeshift plunge pod to use daily.

The mental clarity this gave me is hard to describe - whether after some exercise, after a particularly hard day working from home, home schooling, the heartache of not seeing loved ones – I can honestly say my blue bin saved me many days. The space it cleared in my head, the peace was incredible and to this day nothing compares. I've now upgraded to a whisky barrel but those moments when I can go in I absolutely love and ensure I fit in to most days. As I run I began to notice how much quicker I recovered after a run and a dip in my barrel.

If you have not tried it, don't wait any longer you will not regret it, science also has proven it can ward off Dementia!! As my dad has this awful disease it has made me even more determined to continue my wild dipping.

Finding new places to dip is exciting and no matter where I am I am always wondering where I can go for a dip, you don't need much time either as a wee dip the effects can last for hours. There are not many people who can say they had their photos taken while dipping in a snow covered lake, held huge chunks of ice at Christmas time while in their cossie in the local reservoir or been at the beach when it has been covered in snow! Our wee tribes adventures have been the highlight of many days and nights and the pictures make my family smile, they are proud of my journey and I have even managed to encourage them to try it too. Dipping will make you clear head space just for YOU, you will feel exhilarated, feel truly alive. I am so happy I gave it a go -

You should too you won't regret it.

# Leanne Chlosta, 41, Clydebank, West Dunbartonshire

The Wild in Me

I've been thinking about my wild swimming journey. The how's? The when's? And the Why's. And the answer is simply that there has always been a lot of wild in me. Growing up with my family, we didn't have a lot of money but we lived a life full of fun. My best childhood memories are full of adventures on day trips or camping nights away and even to this day, I can remember specific details about all of these trips. I remember my sister scooping up a jellyfish on an Ayrshire beach and throwing it my way. I can remember the first time I swam at the Devil's Pulpit as a teenager, long before it featured on a television series. Even back then, these trips filled my soul.

Fast forward to now and wild swimming is part of my weekly routine. In fact adventure as a whole is something that I deliberately make time for. It's my self care. In 2012, I became a mum and in 2015, I added another baby to the madness and life was just a blur for the next few years. While I focused on all of the kids activities, both outdoors and in, I can honestly say that I lost a bit of myself. But a change was needed and to get there, I took a huge step out of my comfort zone.

Change is a weird thing. We are professionals when it comes to fearing change especially when it's out with our control when others are making decisions for us. So imagine how fearful it can be to make your own changes in life. I joined an adventure group on Facebook. I joined it thinking that maybe, I'd sit on the side-lines and admire other people's adventures from afar until I started to wonder if I could do that? Could I meet a bunch of strangers for a walk up a mountain? What about my weight? Will I hold people back? I thought about it all until one day I hit "going" on that event invitation and since then, I've never looked back. Within a couple of months of joining this outdoors group, 16 of us, the majority of us strangers to each other, signed up for the Great Glencoe Challenge and our Scrambled Legs team was born. We went on to complete this challenge the following year and we remain friends to this day. Where does swimming fit into this? I hear you ask. Well it comes from the connections made within that team.

Social media has a lot of negativity but it has also brought a lot of people into my life. From joining that group on Facebook, I started to make adventure a regular part of my busy weekly life. Before I knew it, we were going on random road trips all over Scotland. With some of my Scrambled Legs team, we headed to Assynt in the North West of Scotland for a week long adventure. On day two of the trip, we were halfway up the mountain Stac Pollaidh when we heard squealing and laughter echoing in the distance behind us. Looking back, we could see folk running into Loch Lurghainn at the bottom of the mountain. One glance back to each other had us nodding in silent agreement that we were fully committed to doing the same when we descended this mountain. And so, we did. It was baltic!

I can honestly say that life has been exactly like that ever since this trip back in August 2020 and wild swimming has been the main event on every one of the trips that we've had since. From there, I started to receive messages from people on social media, mostly on Instagram, messaging to say that they wish that they could come along. And from then on, I put out open invitations on my stories regularly to see if anyone fancied coming along for a swim.

Welcome the newly formed Mad Piranhas, a group of wild swimmers of all ages, shapes, sizes and ability. People who have found each other on social media through either a mutual love of wild swimming or a true desire to try something new. We swim everywhere and absolutely everyone is welcome to come along. Nobody cares what you wear. Wetsuits, costumes, trunks, whatever. You do you. I'm ridiculously proud of our group which I can honestly say is completely inclusive to all. It's their group just as much as it is mine.

Remember that mum who I mentioned earlier who admitted to losing a bit of herself? Well that's me, Leanne, and I am more than just a mum. I am a wild swimmer who used her newfound love of adventure to truly find herself. Wild swimming makes me feel alive. When I'm in the water, I don't think about anything else. For that time, I am doing something that I love without the pressure of family life, housework and employment. I get to breathe and just be, often surrounded by people who equally understand how that water makes them feel. I also shout and bawl throughout winter and question my life choices but will I ever stop? Absolutely not.

If wild swimming is something that you're curious about then my advice would be to stop waiting and just go. Look out for any local swimming groups on Facebook and Instagram. Pop along to an event, even just to watch and get a feel for the moment. Meet new people. I know it's daunting but they've all been you one day, the new person to the group. When I look at our group now, I can see the new friendships that have formed and the memories that people are making together, both in and out of the water.

My own connection to the water doesn't always happen when I'm in the water. I could be on the water on my paddleboard. I could be island hopping on a ferry. Or I could simply be sitting on my camping chair in my favourite place in the world, Milarrochy Bay. It's not just a physical connection but I reap the mental rewards. It's so good for my own wellbeing and this is the one place where I feel truly grounded. It's my safe place.

Adventure is there for all. The air around us and that wild water is free. I'm fast approaching 42 years old and life just gets wilder and wilder. After all, the wild has always been in me.

What are you waiting for? Let's go!

## Helen Quinn, 57, Newburgh, Fife

I'm a typical cold blooded 'cauld tattie' – I hate being cold and always like to be warm and cosy. In the past I would watch these people at New Year jump into the sea and I genuinely could not imagine anything worse. I was quite vocal about it – thought they were absolute nutters and wild horses would not drag me to do such a thing.

In Autumn 2021, just as we were coming out of lockdown, my two best friends and I were chatting and one of them started talking about open water swimming. Turns out all three of us had been thinking about it – as a child I was a water baby, always in the sea on holiday - but strictly in the summer. We agreed we would try it, but since it was October, it would be far too cold, so we should wait till warmer weather,

Then one of my friends was given a Dry Robe for her Christmas and she texted us and said – why don't we give it a go now? So on Dec 28th 2021 the three of us met at Pittenweem tidal pool. We'd done some research online, bought gloves from Amazon and took the plunge. For exactly 2 minutes. I was terrified (being a cauld tattie) – but it was unexpectedly exhilarating. When we came out I wasn't cold – my skin felt tingling, almost on fire. It was such a buzz!!

The following weekend we met up with Chloe & Linda from the Bonnie Black Swans for a dip at St Monans tidal pool – that was a wild one! Then we started joining the BBS for the regular Monday night swims. The first one, in January 2022 was almost spiritual for me – the sea was dead calm, the night was clear, the stars were shining and the moon was bright. It was breath-taking, awesome, magical. A truly amazing experience. Since then I have swum in seas, lochs, rivers and waterfalls, we've had sunrise swims, camping trips, BBQs and charity events. I did the 12 beaches/12 swims in 12 hours challenge with the BBS – 12 of us completed all 12 swims but were joined by countless others at each stop. And on New Year's Day I joined my first ever Loony Dook – now I was one of the nutters!!

In July of last year I lost my brother after a very short illness - this was a huge shock and extremely painful. Continuing swimming throughout kept me sane and grounded, and provided much needed respite from the grief, if only for half an hour or so.

Wild swimming is a small oasis of time in my day just for me – and each swim is different. On calm days I find peace. On windy, wavy days it is just a hoot jumping the waves. It's always about being outside, part of the landscape and the seasons, a great antidote to the stress of my desk job. I suffer from arthritis, and the cold water is very therapeutic - I always feel amazing both mentally and physically after a swim. Chloe says once you're hooked, every time you see a new body of water you think – how could I| get in there for a swim, and it's absolutely true!

My two friends don't manage to come to the swims very often anymore so it's usually just me – but that's not an issue at all. I have met so many different people – it is such a vibrant, friendly community – there's no judgement , everyone is so welcoming. My Facebook feed is now full of different wild swimming groups and I get FOMO on a daily basis – I would gladly retire and go swimming every day, and that's one of my medium term goals and part of my plan for retirement.

I would, and do, recommend this wholeheartedly to almost everyone I meet – and for anyone who would like to try it but are nervous or scared I would say bite the bullet and just come along. Join the Facebook groups. Just turn up – you will be welcomed with open arms. If you think you might like it, I guarantee you will LOVE it!

## June Ewing, 50, Fife

It was 22nd August 2022, when my daughter and her partner (Jenna and Callum) invited me to join them on their wild swim. My first wild swim. They had been telling me all about how much they'd enjoyed wild swimming and kept encouraging me to give it a go. Another 2 friends, Carol g and Janet King, had also suggested to join their swimming group, Seafield Sinkers. With all this encouragement I felt excited and nervous to get in the water!

We got up at 5am, when my daughter woke me up to get organised for our swim. Waking up at 5am for me was unheard of. My husband actually couldn't believe what he was seeing. With swim boots, a swimming costume, a towel and a hot flask of tea, we arrived at Seafield beach around 5.30am whilst it was still dark! As the minutes went on I was so excited when I seen the sun started to rise, and we made our way down to the water. I was so nervous walking into the water, but I took it slowly and focused on my breathing.

The water was calm, and clear and surprisingly warm! The sun gradually came up, and it was the most amazing morning- the rising sun filled the sky, with vivid bright orange rays. I stayed in for a good 15 minutes, with Callum's guidance. Jenna had just found out she was pregnant with her first baby, so stood on the shoreline taking some photos to capture the moment. When I came out the water, I felt so exhilarated and happy. I felt an instant impulse to go straight back in for a second dip. Who knew wild swimming would become addictive so quickly.

Shortly after, I joined Carol and Janet with the Seafield Sinkers on one of their organised swims. At my first Seafield Sinker sunrise swim, I met Lauri, Tracy and Alison- all wonderful woman. Spending time with this group has helped build my confidence in the water and I always looked forward to joining the group at their sunrise swims.

I never thought at the age of 60 I would find myself wild swimming. After 15 months of swimming, I truly can't imagine my life without it. I'm a yoga and Pilates teacher, and a sound healing practitioner. I now run a Wednesday Yoga and Swim event, at Seafield Beach, which had grown in popularity. The numbers keep growing, and we have a great community. Every Wednesday morning is filled with laughter, fun and great conversations. We have all become firm friends, and everyone in the group is so friendly. Newcomers always comment that the group is very welcoming and friendly towards each other. I've found this is a common theme within the swimming community. Every group or event I have joined has a community feel and welcome you with open arms.

Through the swimming community, I've taught yoga and shared sound healing experiences with many swim friends. I've loved being able to share the benefits that yoga and sound healing can bring to your mind and body with others.

On a personal note, I have suffered depression in the past, and I consciously do make an effort to keep a positive mental attitude. Swimming really does help me to keep a well, calm and clear mind. Being closer to nature helps ground me, and always brings stability and perspective into my life. The energy and joy I gain from the water, never fades. I plan to continue swimming for years to come with the Seafield Sinkers and Fife Floaters, and look forward to making more friendships and memories along the way.

To anyone who is thinking about taking the plunge, my advice would be, the first step may feel scary, but once you have taken that first step into the water, you will never look back.

# Sheila Daly, 70 on my next birthday, Fife.

I grew up on the shores of Loch Fyne and all my childhood was spent on, in, or beside the sea. My summers were spent picnicking and swimming or with my grandpa on the loch fishing from his wee rowing boat the Ruby. Other times we would be beachcombing, gathering shells and sea glass for bad weather projects.

I have always worked full time but in 2022 I retired in order to move house and spend some quality time with my best friend who had been diagnosed with a terminal illness. I, myself, suffer from acute anxiety and when my friend lost her fight for life, I went into a deep depression. For a year I barely went out of the house. I lost touch with friends and spent my days alone with my thoughts. Although I have an amazingly supportive family I made excuses to avoid them, telling everyone I was fine.

I had a deep longing for the joy and freedom I had felt as a child when I was connected to the sea and the water but also so afraid to reach out to new people. I lost all my self-confidence but still I thought more and more about the freedom of the sea.

When I first spotted a post on Facebook from the Fife floaters, encouraging people to take up cold water swimming, I agonised about reaching out. I felt afraid of making a fool of myself in front of strangers. What if I can't do this – will I look stupid -am I too old- what if nobody likes me. How wrong I was, on all counts. I put up a post asking about the group and was contacted by Laurie, who gave me the courage just to try.

On my first swim, I was nervous but the encouragement and support I got from all the girls was amazing. Although the waves were really rough and I spent more time under the water than on it, I felt the joy I had been longing for. I felt instantly re-connected to my soul.

I had no more fear of being judged or not doing well enough and the acceptance and support from my fellow dippers, the laughs and hugs I experienced, along with the exhilaration of being in the sea just lifted me. Although I sometimes don't stay in the water as long as most of group due to old age and decrepitude, cold water therapy has helped to lift my mood and given me back my confidence and given a purpose in life.

I get excited every swimming day and have never felt more a peace than when I'm watching the sunrise as I gently bob on the surface of the sea. I only wish I'd had the courage to do this sooner. I sleep better than ever and just feel physically and mentally so much stronger.

Although not everyone is called by the sea, it has definitely changed my life for the better. My advice would be to join us for tea and chats. You will get to know everyone and No one will push you out of your comfort zone. If the desire is there but the courage is not, then take it at your own pace. It took me months. Once you feel the pull of the sea it will come naturally and give you the biggest rush ever. I am so proud of myself for eventually doing it.   Sheila. X

# Female, 36, Kirkcaldy

Having suffered from anxiety all my life especially social anxiety, which can be very debilitating at times and trying to deal with this holistically as much as I can, I did some research about the benefits of cold water immersion, especially around mental health. I'm also a runner, so when doing my research, I found that it might help with muscle recovery as well as my own mental health. That's when I found some groups on Facebook and Instagram. It was then that I simply decided to go along to one of the events. That was about 1 year ago now.

I've found that when I'm in the water I'm fully present and my racing mind gets a break. This is the best benefit for me as my anxieties can be exhausting at times. I also feel that by being fully present in that moment, with nothing else to focus on other than the water, it gives me a chance to switch off from everything, improving my mood and afterwards with a natural high for hours.

Being in the water makes me feel I can take on the world afterwards as I feel that I have built on my confidence. The entire swimming community has helped a lot with this as everyone I have met has been so lovely. You have no choice but to be a more social person. I love that.
I think that because I have gained so much from joining the groups and taking part and the connections I've made, this all makes it such a great experience. I love sharing that with others.

If you are thinking about doing this in any way, I would say just give it a go. Even if you just go in for a minute and build up and don't put pressure on yourself to stay in for a long time for the very first time. Another good reason to go is to make friends and be part of an amazing community of people.

## Tamara Harrison, 54, Fife, Scotland

I have suffered from treatment resistant major depressive disorder for 30 years and was hospitalised for nearly a decade. I have been "stable" for years, on multiple strong antidepressants. and other resources, such as mindfulness, meditation, yoga/Pilates, good nutrition, resistance training and running/spinning. Sometimes I need a "boost" from electroconvulsive therapy.

I had heard about open water swimming through social media and had thought I wasn't "mad" enough for that! However, after getting benefit for over a decade, I had to discontinue one medication, due to some side effects becoming intolerable and I was terrified because I knew how bad things could get with being so ill before. I immediately thought about any lifestyle changes I could implement, to lessen the blow of "losing" the benefit of the medication and discussed open water swimming with my psychiatrist. He said he'd heard good things and why not try it. So, at the Platinum Jubilee Street Party, in my village, I met a lovely lady who offered to give me a lift to parkrun every week, which I jumped at the chance! She also said she did cold water swimming and offered to help me find out if it was any use for me. She advised re kit needed to try it out and not to invest in stuff till I knew if it was for me. She also was fabulous at making sure I took the water seriously and safety was a big aspect to my initiation.

So, on 20th August 2022 I took my first dook! It was after parkrun, and we went to Lower Largo Beach, where we were able to change in the sailing club, this lessened my anxiety regarding the changing clothes aspect of cold-water swimming! It was 14.5°c, and it was so surprising. I couldn't believe I had done it! Plus, I knew I wanted to do it again. I loved the jumping in the waves.

That was when I then decided it was worth investing in my own "kit". My next dip was at the first "Big Dippy Dook" at Silver Sands, Aberdour on 4th September. It was then, I realised there is more to dipping than just getting wet/cold and the warming up after. Hundreds of people were in the water. Kindred spirits/community. I wasn't feeling judged. It was liberating!

I then decided to do the Penguin Challenge to try and keep dipping over the winter months. This meant I needed to get in the water, covering my shoulders, and out again, twice a month.

In January 2023, I returned from a fortnights holiday in Madeira, to find water pouring from my loft space and ceilings on the floor. I ended up relocating to Kirkcaldy, while work to reinstate the building took place. I was unable to get to St Andrews parkrun and my weekly dips at Eden Springs. So, I decided to look into whether there was a group for me to join in Kirkcaldy. I needed to do 2 dips in March, to complete the penguin challenge.

The Seafield Sinkers, were my first dip in Kirkcaldy. I walked for 30minutes, I don't drive, in my wetsuit, to Seafield Beach. It was busy and there were school children on the grassy area. I was on my own. I knew no one, the dip start time passed, I had just messaged my friend from Eden Springs to tell her no one had turned up, looked into the water and saw a load of people and their tow floats in the sea! I was at the wrong end of the beach! I ran. The mask went on, and I joined them in the water. I wasn't going to not dip now. After all that anxiety and making a complete arse of myself, I waded in telling everyone what an idiot I was. One lady stayed longer than the others in the water with me, so I could at least be in a few minutes.

But, hey! I did it. I knew no one, and still turned up. I certainly surprised myself. I even got a lift from a complete stranger to the Big Dook at Aberdour in April! Now that lady has a very special place in my heart. We were meant to meet, I think.

I started going regularly then. Bonnie Black Swans and Fife Floaters as well as Seafield Sinkers and the subgroup Yogi Sinkers. However, I have been having body temperature regulation problems and not been able to actually swim very often, due to it being too dangerous. But having mental health issues, I recognised it was important to keep the connection and started turning up, as a spotter or bucket minder! I was leaving the house and socialising.

My mental health benefits from being on the beach, hearing the waves, being immersed in nature, away from society and embraced by the love of the dipping community. Our blethers after can be so diverse! From frivolous to extremely deep. We are all talking and listening to people we may not otherwise meet and benefiting each other enormously. Swapping tips re all things in life, be it Mrs Hinch tips, home baking or physical and mental health healing. We are not alone.

On occasions where I have been really unwell and, in a daze, I have been able to turn up, knowing that I would be accepted, and offered kindness to assist in me getting down to the beach to immerse myself in nature, and left to do it, if that's what I needed. Also not having to explain my illness, just accepted and given kindness/hugs. Having this resource has helped me avoid hospital admission, I was so unwell. So, I can only thank the dipping community for everything it stands for.

Don't knock it, till you've tried it. It may change things for the better. Everyone has their own agenda and we are all on different journeys. But we are all the same too, especially when in the water.

Together we are stronger.

# A Huddle of Wildies

A Huddle Of Wildies

At ponds and pools they gather
At sea, the beach and ocean
Hugging mugs and hidden under hoods
Causing a commotion.
By lochs and rivers you'll find them
With cake, laugher and chatter
Under the moon, the stars, the sun or rain
The weather doesn't matter
Bobbing around together
Splashing, swimming and floating
A common interest of freedom
That comes without gloating
A huddle of Wildies is what they're called
And they gather in their clans
With bobble hats and rubber feet
Be sure to wave your hand
If you're lucky enough to see some
Snap a photo or two
They love to share their passion and
They would love to share it with you

LjG

# Dawn Brown, 59, Dundee

I started to swim in Broughty Ferry with the Ferry Dunkers in December 2021 and I so wish I had found the swimming community sooner but I'm glad to be a part of it now. I have even managed to encourage my husband to join in and along with our 12 year old beautiful son. Our son was diagnosed with autism at 2 and a half and he is non verbal and although he doesn't come in the water at the moment, he does come along with us. Part of his autism means that he doesn't enjoy the sand, so this was a bit of a problem at first, but we have since bought him a tent to sit in which helps.

My son's condition has been such a worry for both me and my husband and we often think about who will take care of him when we are no longer here. This takes its toll and has caused us both to have issues with our own mental health.

My own OCD has been exacerbated with the worry. Cold water swimming allows us both to let go of the worries when we are in the water and the connection I feel between the water and nature is so nurturing to the soul. Although I've always been a keen swimmer, I just love smelling the sea air and feeling that the mineral rich water as it soothes my aching body from fibromyalgia.

After the swim sitting on the beach and relaxing whether on my own or with some of the wonderful like-minded people I have met is all the medicine I need.

# Karen Thomson, Age 50, Broughty Ferry.

I have enjoyed being in and around water since I was a child. This started with me playing in paddling pools with friends, catching sea creatures in rock pools on holidays and progressed to swimming in the sea and rivers. As I grew older I tried kayaking, sailing, windsurfing and paddle boarding.

My favourite water activity is swimming, and during the lockdown of 2020 I started swimming regularly with a group of friends on Broughty Ferry beach. We called ourselves The Sunrise Swimmers as we usually met first thing in the morning. The first challenge for me was getting up early and swimming before the sun had had time to warm the day up. However, the coffee and camaraderie afterwards soon warmed me up. We even started swimming in the rain and after dark in moonlight sometimes. We swam often as it was such a lovely summer, and continued into the autumn and winter. We all surprised ourselves at our enthusiasm and resilience and marvelled at how we coped with the dropping temperatures. Our bodies had adjusted to the cooler water temperatures and the coldest swim I did was in water only 3.5C which was classified as an ice swim as it was below 5 C. It was an exceptionally cold winter and I drew the line at swimming in the water when there was ice flowing down the River Tay and the water was only. 0.5 C!

What cold water swimming has taught me is that I am much stronger than I realised, not just physically but mentally too. There is no doubt that getting into cold water is a physical challenge that can take your breath away. What I love is knowing that I have the mental strength to acknowledge this and go in anyway. I find that walking into the water up to my waist helps my body cool down a bit and that if I breathe out as I duck my shoulders under I can avoid the gasp reflex being activated. I find that chatting to friends is a great distraction and helps the minutes I spend in the water to mount up.

One of the best things about knowing I can get into cold water as being able to use that mental strength to help me in other situations by transferring that skill. I am better able to contemplate and deal with other challenges in life such as coping with a time difference when travelling, or not getting enough sleep or being uncomfortable. I can channel that mental ability to cope.

There have been challenges along the way - my first jellyfish sting which was quite alarming and caused pins and needles for 24 hours in my legs even though I was stung on my shoulder. However, I learned to adapt to this risk by covering up more and not going out if there were too many jellyfish around. Unfortunately for my friends they had to put up with my psychedelic swimming suit as I hate wearing black and other options for costumes were limited a few years ago! They'll be pleased that I have a more modest blue suit now.

As a group we had lots of laughs as we hopped around after swimming trying not to fall over as we changed into warm, dry clothes. We did lots of experimenting to try and find the easiest garments to change into and we all invested in dry robes which are an absolute game changer for staying warm especially if it's breezy.

An unexpected bonus of cold water swimming as that my hips, which were waking me up at 5:00 AM as they hurt so much, stopped hurting and I was able to walk without limping. I think this is due to an immune response activated by cold water immersion. In addition, my whole body feels fantastic for several hours after a cold swim - the best way I can describe it is like having a whole body exfoliation on the inside, a kind of fizzy feeling, or like when you have a big drink of cold water on a hot day. It is utterly refreshing and cleansing. I also learned that it's important to warm up slowly as if I showered too quickly I warmed the outside of my body up but my core remained cool for several hours which wasn't pleasant.

Many people swim on my local beach now and there are numerous swimming groups that meet and welcome anyone who wants to join. I love the fact that this activity is open to anyone who can get themselves to a beach or river. There are no rules, the dress code is "anything goes" both in and out of the water. No one cares if you wear a bikini or a wet suit, and the only priority after swimming is to be warm and cosy - style is not a consideration!
I am fortunate to have one friend to swim with regularly now and we can be very spontaneous as we live close to each other and the water. Sometimes our children and other friends join us and it's always a joyful experience and we never regret going in.

I used to swim several times a week which was great while it lasted but now I sometimes don't swim for weeks at a time. Life is busy sometimes and it's fine just to swim when I feel like it and when I have time. I'm very good at saying yes if someone asks me to join them. Occasionally I swim on my own but I'd say it's generally much more fun to do with others. I have tried putting my face under the water but I don't really like it as the cold is unbearable and I lose my bearings, so I save proper swimming for swimming pools.

Wild or cold water swimming isn't for everyone. However, if you are thinking about giving it a go I suggest finding someone to do it with, either a friend or by joining a group, as I think it helps to see and be with others and share the experience. Not only is there safety in numbers, it's generally more fun too! Think about what to change into afterwards – clothes that stretch are a good idea and lots of layers.

My top tip for the winter is to take a hot water bottle in your bag to tuck against your tummy for your journey home. Also, wearing neoprene socks and gloves is an absolute game changer as if your hands and feet aren't freezing you can stay in the water for longer. The main thing is – there are no rules. Go in as often or infrequently as you like for as long or short as you like and if you don't feel like it, don't do it.

Wild swimming is something that is easy to do in lots of different locations, most of which are pretty. I mostly swim in the sea, and swimming in fresh water is a real treat. I keep a swimming costume and towel in my car so I'm always prepared for any opportunity that presents itself, not that I would let not having a costume to wear stop me from taking a dip!!

# Amy Ritchie (aka Mamma Swan) 44, Lundin Links, Fife

It just happened one day. I was walking with a friend and she just naturally fell into talks of swimming in the ocean as we walked a coastal route along Fife's East Neuk. As usual, I approached it the same way I always do with anything that sounds like fun, I jumped right in without any consideration of consequence and asked if I could join her sometime!

My first swim was a winters morning, early February. The air was 2° and there wasn't a whisper of wind. The water looked like glass and the sun bounced off its ethereal surface. There was a still mist in the air and I had no swim gear to protect extremities. But as it was my first swim, I had no idea of what to expect or how to prepare other than a towel and warm clothes for afterwards.

I will never forget that first walk into what would instantly become my 2nd home. I'd say "it was cold" but during those winter months, there really should be another word created for the sensation your skin feels immersed in water below 5 degrees. A noise would seem a more appropriate expression. A low grunt with a haunting extended moan. I was in. I felt sensation in parts of my body I was unaware existed up until that point, and at 40 years old I can tell you that came as a shocking surprise. Every part of my body instantly awoke the way you'd be woken from a sleep by a sledgehammers blow. My hands and feet hurt like hell and every inch of my being was repelling the will to "relax" no matter how many times my dear friend reminded me to do so.

Whoever had assured me "its fine once you're in" was a big fat liar and I was already cursing them under my breath as I slowly slid my shoulders under the icy break.

By this point I had forgotten how to breath, I couldn't feel my body and I was awaiting a nosebleed from my brain exploding a few moments earlier.

"Just breath" I heard her say. So I did. I kept my eyes firmly on my friend who resembled a graceful grinning Cheshire cat. I remember her smiling so hard I could see every one of her teeth. And before I knew what was happening, I was smiling back.

My body had forgotten the shock and pain, and had settled instead into a high vibration of pins and needles all over the surface of my skin. I felt a whoosh of adrenaline, the likes I've only ever felt before in terrible situations like realising I'd lost my purse, or someone jumping out in front of my moving car, or that feeling of falling and hitting the ground just before it wakes you up. Or crippling anxiety, something I had suffered from in the past. That! But surprisingly, I found myself in control of it. I was experiencing well controlled panic. I was able to feel it all without the irrational fear that I would usually feel. It was in that moment that I had my biggest revelation to date and found the reason that would see me entering the water every day thereafter for years to come.

It taught me how to remain calm when my body tried to take over. It taught me how to manage my emotions while feeling heightened adrenaline. It taught me to understand the difference between fear and excitement. And it stole away my anxiety.

From that day on, give or take a day here or there, I make it a point to enter the water every day. All year round, in all weather. I started my group "the swans of a beach" shortly after my first swim, just before COVID hit. Our small, amazing group of swans supported each other through the worst of times, swimming as soon as the opportunity would safely allow. 4 years on and our group of 10, 20, 30 has reached thousands.

Thousands of all ages, abilities, sizes, shape, sex. We are all one and the same when we enter the water. We have formed bonds to last lifetimes and experienced laughter, tears, pain, joy, she takes it all while bathing us in her forgiving glory. We all come together and smile our toothiest grins. Always respecting her, allowing her to heal us.

As a mother of 2 autistic children, it has allowed a way for us to bond in ways we may never have been able to. There is nothing quite so special than snorkelling in the height of summer, moving freely and finding other ways to communicate underwater when we find something exciting. It has brought me so much closer to both my children and has been a tremendous aid with their confidence.

I owe the sea so much. After my first encounter on that winter's morning, I am forever changed. And I would urge anyone who has every considered trying it, to just do it! I promise you.

Its fine once you're in.

# Lorna Green, 50, Central Scotland

When I was in my mid-thirties I had what could only be described as a dumpster fire of a life event. I got sick and the result of that illness there was loss. Loss of my home, my businesses, my relationship and even my sanity for a while. I handled it the only way I knew how, moving to the Maldives and hiding from my perceived failures.

I spent the next decade living, working and travelling around some of the most beautiful places on earth. I was surrounded by white powdery sands, blue seas and skies so clear you'd think you could see all the way to heaven.

I've always been drawn to water even as a child, so it was a natural progression for me to learn to scuba dive during that period eventually becoming an instructor. Spending most of my days outdoors, near water afforded me the strength to find the lessons in that life changing catastrophe years earlier and to manage my ongoing battle with depression that had plagued most of my adult life.

Fast forward to 2020 and my unplanned return to Scotland due to Covid. That year saw me losing the pillars I had so painstakingly rebuilt for myself in the previous decade. My business was gone, I was homeless or so my mum liked to tell people, although I preferred to think of myself a little more romantically as a nomad, a citizen of the world - who just happened to be between homes.

Like many folks the lockdown quickly became something of a prison, exacerbating feelings of isolation and loneliness. It became harder and harder to roll out my yoga mat and my daily walk for an hour was carried out on autopilot. Something had to change but the dark tendrils of depression were taking hold, and a sense of suffocating indifference pervaded my every thought and action. I had never ventured into the waters of Scotland beyond a paddle at Silver Sands in the Summer holidays as a child. I couldn't imagine how this notion of wild swimming in the rain and the mud could be considered fun.

For so long I'd enjoyed the tropical waters and sun drenched beaches of far flung islands - Scotland and its dreich loch sides held little pull for me, or so I thought.

As the grip of the first lockdown loosened, I was able to start seeing clients privately again. One such client lived in Granton in Edinburgh. Each time I met with her she would walk me out after our lesson to go swimming.

One day I asked her where she had to get to, and did she need a lift. She laughed and said oh no, I'm just going over there. My eyes followed as she pointed towards a sea the same colour as the steel grey sky above.

It was my turn to laugh. I wished her luck as we went our separate ways but somehow the idea of dipping in Scotland wouldn't get out of my head. I started to do a bit of research and a few weeks later I asked if I might join her after class. So I took my first dip in the chilly, choppy waters of Wardie Bay. Not perhaps the most beautiful spot on our shores but an unforgettable moment none the less. She and her friends guided me on how to best get into the water, they chatted merrily about being safe and things to look out for as we all bobbed around in the freezing water, a sight to behold with our colourful tow floats and bright swim caps.

I came out exhilarated. I hadn't felt this alive in what seemed like years. I tingled and buzzed and chittered as I quickly pulled on my dry clothes. We sat sipping hot drinks, chatting amiably like old friends, everyone in the group making me feel welcome and safe. I couldn't wait to get in the water again.

After some time dipping sporadically with my newfound friends in Edinburgh, I decided to join a group more local to me. Here, I found my tribe. A crew with just the right amount of madness to make the world a better place.

Since joining West Lothian Dippers almost 3 years ago, I've seen more of Scotland than ever before. I've jumped into waterfalls, got lost on mountainsides and sat on damp rocks with the sun on my skin, aching from laughter.

It even prompted me to take my yoga outdoors, starting a monthly yoga and cold dipping experience at a beautifully secluded beach in South Queensferry. Here I've been able to welcome dippers and yogi's experienced and new to a community that's as much about connection as it is about nature.

The dark shadows still threaten at times, but the water is where I find both solace and strength in equal measure. When you're tired to your very core, you need nature, the sound of waves lapping on the shore, bees buzzing, the breeze on your skin. We are all better people when we stare at the sky and let our minds drift like the cottony clouds above.

I may have resisted my return to Scotland but without it I wouldn't have found a place where I can laugh till I'm hoarse surrounded by folks who are determined to soak up every last drop of joy from the day. I've discovered a resilience I didn't know I had, getting comfortable with being uncomfortable and I've learned to embrace my own seasons, honouring the times when I need to be still and quiet, embracing the periods of energy and exuberance.

I'm Lorna Green a newly minted 50 year old from central Scotland and I'm proud to be one of those women who jumps into lochs and wears onesies outside; who dances by the fire as stories are shared, laughter erupts, and the weight of the day is gently lifted from my shoulders. It's scary to try something new, and step into the unknown but it's also where you flourish.

You don't have to go far, nor do you have to stay in the water for long. In fact you don't HAVE to do anything you don't want to. That's the beauty of this tribe, you are welcome to show up however you want, and you are welcome to participate however you choose.

You deserve to live, to thrive to feel alive in every moment. Take a dip with friends or watch the sunrise in solitude as you sip your hot drink; make time for yourself because this life is short and you deserve the best parts of it.

# Tickle My Toes

"The waves softly call to her, drawing her closer to the shore.
"We want to tickle your toes" they say,
"just a little more".

LjG

# Anna Savage 39, Cruden Bay, Aberdeenshire

I first found out about wild swimming/cold water dipping through my friend Lilia, who was at the time introducing people to Wim Hof and his philosophies. I took the plunge in Loch Fyne at the Goddess Gathering (an event organised by Lilia/Heal Scotland) with other like- minded women and although we did not swim (it was November and I was in a swim suit), the feeling of being in the cold water, surrounded by stunning views, had me hooked. The adrenaline was flowing through my body, I felt euphoric, and I knew at that point that being in the water was going to be very therapeutic for me.

Fast forward a few years and I have recently moved to Cruden Bay in order to support my dad and beloved dog Otto, after the sad loss of my mother, in January 2022, to a short battle with cancer. I am so blessed to live right by the harbour and I knew as soon as I moved that I would be getting in the water as often as I could.

Thankfully I made friends with a beautiful soul, Justine, who lives along the street and she also shared my love for dipping. It is so much easier to go in with someone else, especially if the weather is not great. There is also a 'harbour dookers' Facebook page that allowed me to meet others and swim together at arranged times when the tide is high.

At first I was going in without neoprene gloves or socks/boots however I did invest in these and a float, as they allowed me to swim for much longer (up to forty five minutes at times).

We shared the sea with seals, dolphins and beautiful birds and we have only missed going in to the water on a handful of days since we first met.

Wild swimming has improved my mental and physical health and has helped me deal with grief and stress in a positive way, as well as alleviating some pain in my back that I had at one point.

If you are unsure about whether to dip or not, I would say this… It can be hard getting in at times when it is cold or windy however, you will always feel better afterwards and you can also meet like minded people and form amazing connections. Always make sure you are safe and be sensible and listen to your own body.

If you have pain or mobility issues then wild swimming can really help with this also, as well as increasing your fitness levels. Wild swimming releases endorphins that will leave you feeling on cloud nine for the rest of the day. Try it! You won't regret it. If you are not connected with other swimmers then look for local groups too. Have fun!

# Laurie Gallacher, 51, Dunfermline, Fife

The reason I swim is very simple.
I swim to feel alive. I SWIM BECAUSE I AM ALIVE!
In March 2021 I found out I had breast cancer. Unfortunately it turned out to be stage 4 and aggressive and my chemo was to start immediately.
Nothing had prepared me for this! Not mentally and definitely not physically and so, during the darker days to keep my spirits up I started to make a bucket list of all the things I wanted to do when I "kicked cancer's ass".

Around this same time, one of my friends had posted a pic of herself after a "dook". She looked so happy and invigorated! So number one on that bucket list - WILD SWIMMING.
In the months to come I filled my social media with wild swimming profiles and groups. I read books and I talked to my friend about joining them. Unfortunately I was advised to wait until after my chemo for risk of infection.

So I had to watch from afar until I was given the all clear from my oncologist and when the day finally arrived, my friends, (the girls) decided it would be good to do a sunrise swim.
I set my alarm for 5am, set out all my gear and went to bed as excited as a kid at Christmas. In the morning, I jumped out of bed when my alarm went off (to be honest, I was wide awake anyway), I made up my flask and off I headed into the dark on that cold October morning!

We all met up in the carpark at the beach and as it was my first time (and winter) the girls ushered me into a wetsuit, gloves and boots. We then headed down to the sea as the sun started to pop up from the horizon. I remember thinking how brave the girls were that they only wore swim suits.

We walked straight in, no hesitation. I can't remember exactly how it felt but I can remember the screams followed by laughter and chatter. Then came the sense of calm! I felt totally grounded in the moment and we were only in a matter of minutes. Once we were all dressed and cradling our hot drinks, we watched the sunrise. I couldn't have picked a better morning and I really felt like I could have stayed in that moment forever. The "buzz" stayed with me for days afterwards.

I now swim in just my "cossie" and at every chance possible I'm in the water. Since my first dook, I've also just completed my first ever swim event, covering 750m in Loch Lomond and I plan on doing the 1500m next year.

I'm still kicking cancer butt and receive treatment every three weeks, but every time I feel low I know where to go!

## Female, 56, Scotland

Wild swim and learn something about you.

I discovered wild swimming via a Facebook group that described the experience as 'liberating' and 'great for mental and physical health'. I was curious about the physical benefits as to me, swimming in cold water was only good for catching a cold or worse, drowning! So I did some more research.

The first contact with open water happened on a beautiful August morning in 2019 at Loch Lubnaig. The place was full of experienced swimmers and pentathlon athletes who welcomed us and gave some great advice: 'take it easy', 'it's not about others but just you', 'if you feel warm, it's time to get out', 'if you don't like it, that's fine', 'never swim alone', 'always wear a float'.

Happy to have met nice and caring people, I took a deep breath and started walking into the water. It was 'cold' to me, later, I will realise it was not that cold but still, I remember it as being 'freezing' to what experienced swimmers would laugh at, as in August, the loch water was, that day at 18°!

Intuitively, I understood that breathing was key to wild swimming, and I focused on in-breath and out-breath, like in Yoga, massaging with water my arms, tummy and neck and continue walking until I was fully immersed. Within minutes and without thinking I was 'part' of the water, the nature, my surroundings and it changes something deep inside me, something I still cannot explain or word for that matter. I believe I stayed no more than 10 minutes but to me it appeared like hours.

The temperature shock afterwards was a bad experience as no one told me about that. I shivered for the rest of the day, feeling the cold taking over my body, deep to the bones and each tissue. It was not painful but made me feel dizzy and loosing contact with reality and I realised how easy it would be to just let go and drown should that happen while in the water. Still, I needed to go back. 'Need' is the verb that best described the urge to go back, get cold to the point of not feeling my thighs, tummy, back and neck, but get back to the water, immerse myself there, swimming slowly, breath-in 1,2,3, breath-out 1,2,3, look around, the gentle silvery waves coming from the opposite bank, the swimmers around getting ready to cross the loch, women's babbling, laughing at each other and themselves. Swimming away from people, enjoying the sun and floating gently until I fully blended with water, just being there, clearing the mind, cleansing the soul, breath-in, breath-out.

With time, I learned how to manage the cold water shock once out, by simply changing as fast as possible even to risk of showing part of my anatomy to people betting on when the towel might drop, drink hot drink and keep moving. I always listened to my body and managed a technique of getting in and stayed in without thinking about the cold, yet still feeling it as I was fully aware of my environment. As the experienced swimmers said, 'it's about you, no one else', I understand now what they meant; wild swimming is not a competition against others and certainly not against us. Wild swimming is a way to connect with nature, but more important with our true self, the self we keep deep inside, hidden and protected.

With time, I felt brave enough to swim in the open sea and loved it. A very different experience from a loch, first the taste of water then the currents and of course fauna. Sea is overall warmer than lochs and it's nice during the winter as no need to break the ice for a swim. Then, natural pools in hills were also a beautiful discovery with some unexpected natural Jacuzzi effects. Natural pools are places hidden that, selfishly, I tend not to share as I could see with years of 'wild' swimming the effects on the water and fauna with higher concentration of pollution where humans decided to immerse themselves.

So early in my 'swimming' I advocated for not wearing make-up, body lotion, deodorant or the likes when swimming in open water, and also advised others to check the currents when sea swimming.

Swimming benefitted my physical health as I noticed I had no cold for the time I swam but had to stop in 2021 when my husband was diagnosed with a terrible illness. For months, I focused on him but I could feel that my health was not so good as before. Once better, my husband drove me back to a loch and it felt like a re-birth; I swam for a long time, cleansing my flesh from the hospital smell, clearing my soul form the worrying and uncertainties ahead. With time, I went more regularly I felt the immediate benefit as I slept better and felt 'me' again.

Nowadays, a loch to me is a safe place, where I can relax, where I feel protected and nurtured. Listening to birds' chirping or getting splashy silvery waves in my face as a wake-up call that life means being present, in the now. Not in what could or should have happened but there and now.

Swimming or dipping as we tend to say helped me build a better physical endurance and health; it kept me afloat when all my world was overturned, it prevented me from drowning in anxiety and stress.

Anyone will have a special relationship to nature and each of us have a different way to connect with it, whether hiking, painting, singing, swimming. To me, dipping/swimming has become more than a physical exercise, it is linked to surroundings and seasons, dipping during a full Moon brings a new dimension to such connection too.

As the experienced swimmers said 'it's not about the others' and this is it. It's about you and your deepest thoughts. Whether you want to try for health benefits or out of curiosity, it will change something in you that might not be easy to express, but it will make you learn something, whether you like it or not.

# Jan Buist, 56, Fife Scotland.

I moved back to Fife after 30 years working and living in England and have established, over the last three and a half years a daily routine of a swim in the sea. When I think back to when my adoration of being in the sea began, it was probably when I was small and paddled carefully at the edge. I was a non-swimmer until the age of twelve but would still dream that one day I would enjoy the waves properly and with age and confidence, my travels abroad allowed my swimming in open water to become a longed for activity, but it was confined to holidays only! I never dreamt that swimming in UK waters could be considered a normal daily practice.

The attraction for me to settle here on my return to Scotland was heavily driven by the proximity to the sea and beach. It never occurred to me that there would be, in our community, a group of likeminded people who would happily encourage me to join them for a swim. I met this wonderful small number of people through walking my dog by the beach.

After being introduced I initially fed myself the self-doubts that quite possibly the majority of first timers do. Am I going to be strong enough to keep up? Are they all really technical swimmers? Do they all swim really fast?, What if I can't stay in the cold water for long? How far out will they swim? Do they all wear specialist kit?

Smiling faces and a reassurance from them that everyone is different plus, thank goodness, my inner child shouting to me, "just get on with it". I did it! I took my first swim in Fife! I have never stopped since the first glide through the waves at Lower Largo. I was mesmerised and thrilled at the absolute high that I experienced! There has not been a single swim in the last three and a half years at 7.30am that has been regretted. Come rain, hail, snow or sunshine we swim with respectful care. Each swim has brought an unequalled awareness of being alive.

My recognition of nature's force lifting me from the daily grind and elevating me to a carefree weightless freedom is unrivalled. This takes me to a place where I can spill any inner frustrations or upset with no judgement. The sea allows my inner child to squeal and laugh at its antics. Its unpredictability and constant changing remind me that nothing stays still for long, so I should enjoy what I have and let it take any lingering doubts or upsets away!

I was diagnosed with Passive Remittent MS nearly 20 years ago and I feared that my life would change for the worse! It has indeed changed me. I have found a new appreciation of my life simply by letting the cold water wrap me up, wake every tingling nerve in my body, sharpen my vision of the rising sun and the lingering moon, revel in the hidden secret that only the start of every day holds when so many are still tucked under the duvet.

The sea doesn't judge me. It doesn't make any imbalance feel uncomfortable, it doesn't care if my memory and coordination are not working nor does it mind how fast, slowly, powerfully or indeed how long I swim for. It gifts me every day just by waking me. There is no medicine that can compare.

There are many swim groups throughout the entire UK. Our small group is part of 'Swans of a beach.' You will find there are many pictures and written pieces that have been inspired by my swims over the last three and a half years. There are also many other perspectives for you to browse through. They will offer reassurance, confidence and safety.

Each swimmer of every group will have a unique perspective of what this experience brings. There should be no judgement. Your open water experience is unique to just you. It is an offering of time that can be short to allow a brief paddle or longer for a swim, but the thrill and exhilaration of trying will lift you for the day. Strive to find your inner child, we all have one. Free it to enjoy the day and allow the weights of an adult life to leave you for a short time.

# Lesley Henderson, 55, Leven, Fife

My wild swimming (dipping) journey started about 1 ½ years ago after a spur of the moment jump in the sea. I just couldn't believe how happy I felt and I hadn't laughed so much in such a long time, so, simply from then I continued to dip as often as possible and in all weathers.

I feel this experience helped while I was grieving from the loss of my dad and realised it did wonders for both my mental and physical health too.

When I'm in the water it brings out my inner child. I feel like I'm somewhere else and can switch off to everything that's going on in my world. I feel calm and at peace and really, I just have good fun bobbing about in the water or jumping about in the waves, not to mention, it's a good work out.

I really love a sunrise dip as I do feel that being in the water, watching the amazing colours changing in the sky and the sun rising as it glistens and sprinkles lovely patterns over the water is truly magical. Mesmerising. Euphoric even. It is the best start to any day and really worth the early rise.

I do like all seasons but feel in autumn/winter I get more of the cold water benefits. That anticipation as I brace myself to get in is the hardest part but truly worth it once you're in the water and as for the winter drying and getting changed, well this is done at maximum speed. Once you've dried off though and dressed and cosy (thawed out is a closer description) a that's the best part of all. That's when you get to enjoy your hot cuppa and a sweet munch of some sort.

There's always cakes and biscuits and usually lots of home baked stuff from various dippers too, which are always tasty.

That is when I feel the true great benefit. I'm happy and high on life. I have a clear focused mind-set and at peace with everything. I'm content.

Dipping for me is like a total reset as I feel as light as a feather. Any aches I had have gone, and I'm just full of energy. This can sometimes last for couple of days after too. Another bonus is that I love full moon dipping and another way to reset. I just love watching the moon as it glistens over the water.

I have met lots of lovely people along my dipping journey and had plenty great fun times and will continue my dipping adventures. Give it a go. You never know where it might take you.

# Michaela Street, 53, Scotland

No Way! Absolutely Not! Not A Chance! I am that fifty three year old person Michaela (Mitch) Street who dislikes the cold and water. I also suffer with Raynaud's Syndrome, a circulation problem which causes extremely painful fingers and feet when they get cold and it takes an age to warm them up again. Would I ever consider Wild Swimming? No way, absolutely not, not a chance. These were my consistent words when ever asked about wild swimming it was simply not and never was on my radar.

I first heard about wild swimming a number of years ago when listening to the Reverend Kate Bottley on Radio 2 She would be so enthusiastic about it, and I did think it sounded wonderful the way she described it, especially how it helped with her health and wellbeing. I even felt a little envious as I thought it was something I would never get to experience. I thought I would actually hate being wet and cold and the changing "faff" wow, there was just no way. So what changed? Grief and the decline of my mental health is what changed.

Grief has been a large part of my life for so long after losing beautiful babies, two of my closest friends and then my hero, my Dad who passed away suddenly whilst away on holiday after years of fighting the big C.

Around the same time as my Dad's passing, we then entered into the world changing like we had never known it with the pandemic. This left my Mum very alone and isolated and although I couldn't be with her (me in the Highlands of Scotland and Mum in Bolton, Lancashire) she lent on me over the phone She was extremely depressed and it was a time of so much distress for me, feeling totally helpless.

Sadly my Mum took poorly and as Covid was with us she went into hospital alone, to be told alone that she had pancreatic cancer and had roughly three months to live. I was honoured to grant her the wish of staying at home and so I travelled down to care for in the comfort of her own home. Her suffering was horrendous to experience and when she passed, my grief took over my life. I was struggling severely with my mental health feeling very depressed at such a huge loss and consumed by the whole experience. I couldn't find anything to help me cope other than audio books during the night to try and stop the sadness and thoughts taking me over.

Four months dragged on and a New Year's Dip was being advertised at Loch Insh near where I lived. It had become a topic of discussion among my friends, but again it was a resounding no from me when my husband asked on New Year's Eve did I want to go.

Then that New Year's Day 2022 morning something in me changed.

As I sat at the window and watched my neighbours coming back home from their dip, wearing their changing robes and bobble hats, one even being carried by their partner from the car, I just felt this urge, to this day I have no idea why, but I turned to my husband and simply said "I am going to do it". "What?" he said..."On my birthday on January 8th I will go to Loch Insh and dip!!"

So on the day I turned 52 I wore a neoprene short sleeved

top and a swim skirt. I borrowed boots and gloves along with a bobble hat and I walked straight into a snowy Loch Insh and dipped. It was the most empowering moment ever. Yes, it was an emotional few moments but I took the feeling of peace and nature that surrounded me into my mind and soul and just embraced the experience fully. Cold and all.

That was me hooked. Now, I go every day if possible and sometimes I double swim. I have even since that day, ditched the neoprene and swapped it out for skins (just a swim suit), although I do still have to wear socks and boots along with gloves (diving mitts in winter) otherwise I would really struggle. I am also now known for my 50s style, colourful floral hats which I also make for fundraising through my own Facebook Group Craft Cottage.

For some advice…Apart from the absolutely essential tow float, I practised beforehand with different items of clothing to see what would be easiest to change into when my skin was cold and damp. I knew I would panic otherwise and needed to heat up quickly because of my condition. Mastering this technique is as essential as your tow float.

So, I now wear exactly the same clothes every time and have my routine I follow when I come out of the water. I pack my bag in the order I will be putting on my clothes and always leave my feet in my boots until last. Then its hot water bottles and gloves with a hot chocolate to warm up.

It does take me over an hour before I warm up afterwards, but I am sensible, and I do not stay in the water too long. I listen to my own body at every swim/dip. With the water temperature and the changing weather conditions outside the water being the most important factor for me.

I have also recognised that my own body can also be different daily, if I am tired or if I haven't had my warm porridge and hot drink close enough to my entering the water or I am in a bad place mentally. These all have a major impact on how I can cope with the cold.

I can honestly say it has changed my life though. I love the whole experience from organising my bag, to entering into the water, to enjoying the feeling, the peace, the oneness of being with nature right up to the feeling of my body warming up from the inside out bringing so much awareness of my own body, mind and spirit and now, when someone asks me to go dipping, my answer is….Absolutely! Yes!! Get me into that water and I need to be in the water!!

I know now that if I am ever struggling it is the only place to be, in the water with my eyes closed and feeling the water on my body and the feeling as I swim. To be surrounded by cold water and nature, listening to bird songs or the waves brings inner peace. A place I can go to be quiet, maybe talk to the sky and sometimes a place I go to scream! I get all my anxieties out then spread my arms and glide through the water and feel I can breathe again.

I am very fortunate to enjoy the beautiful fresh water Lochs of the Highlands and the salty seas of the Fife Coast. I feel I experience four different kinds of Wild Swimming.

Firstly the Lochs give you the peaceful surrounding of the lush forests, birds flying above you sometimes I am lucky enough to be joined by an osprey and of course the Cairngorm mountain range so a place where I truly feel at one with nature and peace. My favourite is Loch Vaa followed by Pityloulish, Insh and Loch Morlich.

Secondly The Lochs give me my most favourite, that of an Ice dip. Breaking the ice and slowly submerging as I concentrate on my breathing.
From the person who said absolutely not a chance, I hate the wet and cold, no way, to now loving the water the colder the better. I love the sensation of my skin tingling it makes me feel alive and raises all my senses. It certainly calms my mind and takes away some of those dark thoughts within.

Thirdly the buoyancy of the sea and all five of my senses being used.

I love being in the sea feeling it all around me, tasting the saltiness on my lips, the smell of the sea along with the fish from the creels, hearing the waves, seeing the huge expanse of the sea and sky and how big the universe is and it helps my mental mind to see the grandness of nature and that there are so many others who like me are struggling and many more going through even harder times. It makes me feel grateful to be alive.

The fourth includes as the third but there are two different experiences one when I swim in the sea at my favourite harbour and the two bays in Crail or the coastal tidal pools my favourite being Pittenweem as these are generally calm sea swims. So the fourth experience is in the crashing waves at St. Andrews at least once a week if lucky or Crail, when all you can do is laugh, jump, fall over and laugh again.

Please if you have ever thought about trying it I say give it a go. I can honestly say if I can do it then anyone can give it a try. If you are struggling with your mental health there is no better prescription. Always stay safe, many go with groups which are so encouraging and motivating, they help you whilst in the water but also it's the friendship when out of the water and getting changed. It can help to give you that wee push you sometimes need to get motivated to go and do it with a time arranged and company and once you are in the water you are so grateful to of pushed yourself.

I personally enjoy being with dippers in Aviemore and the locals of Crail occasionally however I have found for my own mental health and now this year 2023 with a health disability that I far more benefit from going in the water alone with a spotter on the side, sometimes when I am not in a good place I need to be in the water right there and then and waiting till later in the day doesn't help me as it causes me more distress. I sometimes just need to be alone and enjoy the peace so I can concentrate on myself and not have to feel I need to be wearing my mask faking happiness and joy as so many of us do. I feel I need the quietness and head space and just be at peace in the water. The water brings me stillness with the sensation and nature and the cold along with my breathing brings awareness of my body, mind and the life I have to life.

Whichever you choose you will not regret it and your mental health will certainly not regret it but benefit from it.

Wild Swimming?      Absolutely Yes. YES YES YES.

# Self Love

Self-Love

Hold on to the memories
And make many more
Let go of the old and messy
To clear the way for the new
Push on when things are tough
Or rest in the shadows, you will get there.
Grow more when you're uncomfortable
You are always learning
Love yourself when you look in the mirror
You're beautiful.
Believe it.
You are capable of doing anything
So just go for it
And remind yourself everyday
You are perfect
See what others see

LjG

# Catrina Kivlin, 63, Perth, Scotland

Since I was young I always swam in the sea or rivers. I remember on holidays always wanting to be in the water and as my mum couldn't swim, she was often reluctant to let me go in. It was in fact my uncle and auntie who taught me how to get in the water safely when I was about 3 or 4 years old. My mum didn't learn to swim properly until she was 65 and it was myself who taught her. Something I feel honoured to have been able to do for her.

I have some incredible memories of beaches up and down the British coastline and school holidays were often spent in the open air pools or at Portobello, North Berwick, Dunbar and Port Seton. I remember it was still really cold, there wasn't much in the way of facilities but I loved it regardless.

I have a distinct memory of sledging as a child and at the bottom of the hill was a burn. As I was heading down the hill, I couldn't control the sledge and I went right into the burn at the bottom. I thought it was absolutely amazing. I was freezing cold but I felt incredible, maybe that's where my journey really began after feeling the buzz from that experience. I must have been about 8 or 9 years old at the time.

As a teenager, anywhere we visited, if there was water, I was in it. Even if I didn't have a swimming costume, I would just strip off down to my bra and pants, in for a swim and then put my clothes back on afterwards. Everybody thought I was mad.

I don't know why, I just have an infinity for water.

Another lovely memory for me is during my pregnancy, the day before I gave birth to my son I was actually swimming in the sea with my massive bump. I loved it.

Over the last 20 years my friends and I have often hired a cottage for New Year (specifically near the sea or near a river) and we would do our New Year dook. Although we were never in longer than 5 minutes or so, it was such a great way to start the New Year. The coldest water we have experienced doing this was in Brora, when it was minus 13 on the beach. The sea was actually frozen and it was the most amazing feeling I've ever had.

Around 10 years ago I came back up to Scotland and was given the news that I had fibromyalgia and hypermobility syndrome. Although my hypermobility has been with me since birth, its only in the last 10 years that I had been feeling pain with it. Part of my treatment for this condition involved medication which unfortunately caused a massive reaction. This reaction led to me having a stroke.

After my stroke, I couldn't really swim for a while but I did gradually build my confidence back up in a swimming pool. I then found somewhere that actually had an outdoor facility and a spotter.

The Merthyr Mermaid played a big part in my recovery and inspiration as well, giving her the courage to just go for it again and I've found now, that when I am swimming and especially in the cold weather, I don't have pain for about 2 hours after getting out of the water. I feel more like the person I used to be and to not be in pain 24 hours a day was brilliant. I didn't feel I was in pain however it was usually followed by extreme tiredness.

For me though, this fatigue didn't matter because I was pain free for those 2 or 3 hours.
Not only did the cold water help with my physical health, but it gave my mental health a bit of a break too.

At the same time as my diagnosis and stroke recovery, my husband was going through a lot of complex PTSD issues. This led to my own struggling too.

Without realising, swimming has actually helped me cope with this. Putting me in a different place mentally when I swim. I talk to other people as well, but not necessarily about my home life or struggles. It just gives me a sense of peace and tranquility and with it being do cold I have no choice but to concentrate on breathing in the water. Giving my mind a break from stress thoughts.

A lot of my friends that are non swimmers think I am absolutely mad to do this, however they do admire me for it. I have seen so many people feel apprehensive about going into the water but once they've done it, they come out and they feel really good. They keep going back for more.

Wild swimming has really helped me throughout my life for various reasons. Not all that have been mentioned here. The list of reasons is just too long.

I intend on continuing to do it though, until I can't do it any longer.

Cheers, Catrina

# Lorna Finlay, 64. Fife, Scotland.

I'm Lorna, a 64 year young retired Advanced Neonatal Nurse Practitioner. I retired in 2022 and now just do a couple of very part time jobs as a Celebrant and Aesthetics Nurse. This leaves me with lots of free time to kill. Well that's in between my voluntary work at a children's charity and the church and also looking after my grandchildren.

I first heard about the joys and health benefits of wild swimming from my friends and my sister who shared their excitement with me and following a programme on the Blue Planet with Catherine Kelly, I understood that it could improve our cardiovascular fitness, release mood enhancing endorphins as well as assist with muscle building and bone density. This was already appealing to my better nature but what I didn't realise was that wild swimming could also boost my skin cell regeneration which slows as we age. Being in my 60s, my skin was now very dry and cracked, on the soles of my feet had especially been a problem area for me and I had been using moisturising creams daily. Since I started swimming however, I now use them less frequently.

In addition to the attractive health benefits, I soon found out that wild swimming would also bring me into to contact with an incredibly diverse group of amazing people who also enjoy this wild swimming malarkey. The social aspect is quite joyful and I am delighted to have met such a nice group of both women and men.

I love the fact that being in the sea can build resilience and pleasure in the endurance from the bracing North Sea and its many moods and as a Christian I find renewed delight in my

Creator as I witness the stunning but dependable sunrises and the scenery that augments them.

When I joined the Seafield Sinkers and Fife Floaters a couple of months ago I attended some of the early morning swims as well as the evenings and have enjoyed the early morning ones especially, however, with the weather becoming less inviting and the mornings increasingly darker I may move to the mid morning swims. I still want to swim twice a week at least so will do this when I can.

Having now lived in Kirkcaldy for over 40 years, I am delighted to find that the Sinkers and Floaters wild swimming mostly takes place off Seafield Beach which is just a couple of miles from where I live. Although I have swam at Dysart which is very stony and Leven, a long and sandy shoreline. Pittenweem is another favourite, which is a n outdoor tidal pool, though it's quite a walk from the car park and lots of steps if you have any difficulties with walking and it's also stony, but not as much as Dysart.

To date I wear just a swimsuit and goggles along with my tow float. My goggles are particularly helpful for when we are just wave jumping as I don't like sea salt water in my eyes. I also wear neoprene gloves and water shoes. I have a changing robe for afterwards and have just bought a dryrobe and wetsuit for the extreme winter.

Going into my third age and assuming I may have 25-30 years God willing to live, I want to be as fit, independent and able as possible while enjoying new adventures. I decided to buy a wee camper van to go exploring and may wild swim on holiday around the UK and maybe even abroad.

It's my hope that sharing my journey with you, that you too find the courage to just go for it.  Maybe we will meet in the water one day.

# The Light

The Light

Dark were the shadows of her mind with thoughts echoing into the depths of the abyss
She stood there on the cusp, with her hands over her heart.
Holding and hoping for a glimpse of happiness.
Soon the sun will rise and burn through the sticky, suffocating mist.
Dispersing the haar and gifting her just enough time to shed those heavy layers of her soul, letting go.
Revealing to her once again the tenderness.  Lighter and in harmony.  Revitalised.
Nourished and free.

LjG

## Chloe Batchelor, 31, Kirkcaldy, Fife.

Hi, I am Chloe and I am one of the 4 members who started the wild swimming group "the Bonnie Black Swans", which was formed 2 and a half years ago. It started months before we actually took our first swim following a conversation between my mum Lynn and her friend Susie. They had been talking about how they would love to try it. This was however, only a conversation then, and it wasn't brought back up again until my mum was walking along the beach catching up with another friend Linda who shared the same enthusiasm.

Back then, I personally didn't know much about wild swimming and I hadn't heard much either, but when mum asked if I wanted to try it with them I thought why not, I'll try anything.

The four of us then arranged our first dip on a cold sunny day in March, at Pathhead sands in Kirkcaldy. I had on my aunties wet suit, a pair of old thin water shoes, no gloves and no tow float and it was freezing! But we were all on a high and I remember sitting on the beach after talking about how great we felt! After just one swim we were already talking about starting a Facebook group, at that time we hadn't heard of any other Facebook groups for wild swimming, so that evening after our swim Linda started up the Bonnie Black Swans Facebook page.

2 and a half years have passed since then and our page has grown do much. I still love getting into the water as much as I did when I first went in and I can honestly say it has changed my life. Wild Swimming has definitely helped me

with my health, certainly with my physical health as I walk dogs for a living and have always suffered from pain in my lower back and legs. The cold water has helped immensely with easing that for me. But, the water has also helped with my anxiety as I feel it really clears my mind and gives me a feeling of being alive.

As well as physical and mental benefits for me, there is also the social aspect of it. I have had 2 and a half years of fun, laughter, new friends and the best memories ever! Weekly swims, weekend day trips around Scotland, swimming camping trips, meals out, nights out, challenge days and charity days. I just love that like minded people come together to do things they love and are just enjoying life - that's my real buzz.

For anyone wanting to try wild swimming, I can't recommend it more.

# Tracy Robb, 53, Leslie, Fife.

At the time of writing this, I'm approaching 54. I'm also a mother of 2, step mother of 3 and a crazy Nana to another 3. I live with my partner Chris. I was first asked to share my "journey into swimming" story at the Big Mahoosive Dook in April 2023 by the author of this book Laurie and i was so nervous. Afterwards though, it felt amazing to have shared my experiences and also listen to others too so I'm happy to have been asked to contribute in this book as well.

My journey really started a good few years prior to swimming and I feel it's important that I give you the back story because it really does contribute to why I swim now. So, a couple of years ago, I found myself really struggling with lots of issues. There had been so many things all happening in my personal life, my work and my health, all at once and I began to spiral. I was feeling so overwhelmed with it all and wasn't coping. So much so that I had started taking panic attacks.

The stress was also playing havoc with my digestive system and so, I was becoming increasingly unwell before each shift at work and as I felt that I was being victimised and bullied at my workplace, it was just adding to that stress.

Whilst I was struggling with this, the Menopause decided to take hold and I was so confused and exhausted with all these emotions running through me all at once. I'd be angry and tearful all the time and I felt like I was losing myself as well as everyone around me. I started to think that I would be better off not alive. I wasn't me anymore and yes I contemplated suicide.

I would walk home from work and at the bridge I crossed over on the way, I'd look over and wonder if I'd survive the jump. I had similar thoughts more and more frequently and knew I had to get help. I was breaking down and didn't know how to fix myself or my relationship with my partner too because obviously it was affecting him.

I called the doctors from work and I fell apart. He listened and he immediately placed me on HRT. This helped to start with but until work issues were also resolved, nothing was really changing. My menopause story is ongoing and I'm still doing what I can to try and fix that.

As for work, well, in January 2022, I quit. I completely broke down at work for the last time and I just did it. I quit there and then!! Nothing had been improving. Not even after voicing my concerns with my area manager and for the first time ever in my life I requested a sick line from my GP.

I was fortunate enough to find another job only weeks later and yes it's still stressful but I have a better balance now, between work and my personal life. Leading me into my swimming.

I've known Allison for nearly all my life and Laurie for the last 6 years. We came together properly during lock down and met up regularly for long walks, just enjoying each other's company and being out in nature. We'd chat about our lives and support each other through whatever was happening at the time. It was around April 2022 when the subject of swimming in the sea was mentioned, by Laurie of course, but it was only briefly discussed and then brushed aside again, until 13th July 2022 when we 3 ladies decided to do something about that thought.

It was the Full Buck Moon and the beautiful Swans of a Beach welcomed us along to their special evening swim. Packed with everything except the kitchen sink, we travelled to Lower Largo with huge enthusiasm, excitement and a big bunch of nerves too! No fancy gear, no proper shoes, no gloves, nothing except ourselves! What an experience! My journey and our real journey as 3 friends had started. From there we tried to swim as often as we could and wherever we could. We joined ALL the groups but mainly based ourselves at Seafield associating with the Sinkers, in Kirkcaldy Fife.

Events were created but sometimes our work patterns meant we'd miss some. I totally rely on 'my girl's' Allison and Laurie for transport, so if they couldn't go, neither could I. However, Sunrise was ideal. We'd head off and be in the water very early in the morning and that's how Sunrise Sinkers became a thing. Every sunrise swim is special and not one is the same as the other. To see that beauty that early in the morning, starting the day that way is just fantastic.

Don't get me wrong, there are some mornings where I wake and decide not to go, then I see the pictures and my regret kicks in. I always say "you never regret a swim", but you do regret not going sometimes as I often hear myself saying "I'm so glad I decided to come".

The journey continues though and the Sunrise Sinkers continued through the winter, and boy was that tough!! But we did it. Together, we supported each other and gave each other a gentle nudge in the mornings when it was pitch dark and freezing cold. We got there and we are so proud to have achieved this.

Then, only on the 5th April 2023 us 3 girls who had no idea how fabulous wild swimming would be back in July 2022 created our own group, the Fife Floaters. We continue to grow more and more. Hopefully inspiring and helping others on their journey.

See, for me personally, swimming has been my saviour. It's given me my identity back. My smile, that was lost has returned. I see this smile in the many photos that are taken and even my daughter comments by saying "Mum, you look so happy", and I am happy. It's been so beneficial for my physical health, relieving joint pain in my ankle and lower back and as for my mental health, well what I call 'resetting my brain' has definitely alleviated my stress levels. My smile is testament to that.

People call us crazy but until they or you take that first step into that water then how do you know that it won't benefit you? I and many others will be here to help you make that first experience wonderful.

Come join us.

# Annemarie Munro-Fleming, 43, Inverkeithing, Fife.

If you had told me 6 months I would start (and continue) Wild Swimming I likely would have laughed in your face. However here I am two months after my first outdoor swim and I am currently swimming every day for the Maggies Dip a Day in October challenge.

My name is Annemarie and I am 43 and live in Inverkeithing, Fife with my husband and 16 year old.

So what made me start wild swimming I hear you ask? I had seen a few friends try it during lockdown but it never really appealed to me. When my neighbour and friend Karen started swimming in the summer I could see the positive impact it was having on her mental and physical health. I was full of admiration for her and that flicked the on switch in me. I knew I would probably benefit from it but the timing just wasn't right. You see I was signed off work with stress related illness as my Dad was in hospital recovering from his first round of chemotherapy after being suddenly diagnosed with acute myeloid leukemia at the end of June. Life at that moment entirely existed of visiting him in hospital and supporting my Mum with general day to day tasks.

After an 8 week spell in hospital and battling an infection after treatment my Dad was allowed home. A few days after he got out I had what can only really be described as a stress induced extreme anxiety/panic attack. Although at the time I thought it was a stroke. It was one of the scariest experiences I have ever had and the first person I contacted was my neighbour Karen who rushed over to check me over. Once checked out by ambulance staff and A&E I was resting at home the next day when she suggested I went with her for a paddle. Right there and then I decided to try it and after that initial cold water "take your breath away" shock I was in and swimming in the sea where I managed a full 30 minutes!

Thing was exhilarating and invigorating and from that moment on I was entirely hooked. Since then I am regularly going swimming 4 or 5 times a week. I go every Tuesday and Thursday evening with Karen and another friend Lyn and we are often joined by some other lovely ladies at Aberdour Silver Sands, we have nicknamed ourselves the "Divit Dippers" and you can find us on Facebook. Other times I have swam with my husband or on a nicer day just myself and have enjoyed swims at Lochore Meadows and more recently St. Monan's tidal pool.

I started off swimming around 25/30 minutes but that has been decreasing as the weather gets a bit cooler. I've grown to value that time so much. I feel so much calm and inner peace when I am in the water and any aches and pains or internal overthinking I have just float away. Although I am very early on in my own wild swimming journey I am looking forward to exploring different areas of Scotland in the coming months and years as I can fully appreciate and value the benefits it has on my physical and mental health and wellbeing.

Divit Dippers –
https://m.facebook.com/groups/828297698752158/?ref=share
Tiktok- @Anners1

Instagram – adventures_with_anners

## Harriet Hay, 57, Leven, Fife

My Soul becomes awake, Beach life and me.

I have always lived by the Fife coast (Leven beach) and have so many good memories of family fun days and sandy sandwiches as a kid, or as a teenager with my friends having fun as teenagers do. Then, as an adult, I remember taking my own children and now my grandchildren. I've had many walks along the beach with my dogs or just sat in the car. Rain, hail, sunshine or snow, drinking coffee with my hubby watching the waves and soaking in the atmosphere feeling relaxed and calm, just enjoying the peaceful moments.

Despite all the fun times and everlasting memories, I would still prefer to swim in the local swimming pool, which I love and get many benefits from. We all know there has been much study and research over the years into swimming and the health benefits.

However, during a time when all swimming pools, gyms and other facilities were closed, wild swimming became a choice for many and now it has become very popular. I'm mostly hearing now, that exposure to the cold water and sea swimming especially helps with mental health, menopause and pain and I would agree with this fully as I've seen these benefits myself since I started. I'd like to share some more about my own personal experiences. Taking in to consideration, health and safety first, you own ability's and never taking the Sea or Mother Nature for granted. (SAFTY

FIRST ALWAYS).


The neuron's in my brain went from mumbo jumbo to thinking straight and clear. It was like a spring had just sprung straight.

The pain from body would leave.
I felt the age of my soul which is ageless, just being free in the sea.
My eyes became wider and brighter.
I felt one with the sea, like I belonged.
I felt like I could connect with the sea life, I would snorkel and take photos/video.
I would IMAGINE I was swimming with mermaids who were my invisible mermaid soul sea sisters, they would help, guide and protect me when I was swimming alone.
I became more creative, imaginative.
I became more confident of the sea, But also aware of do's and don'ts, when and where, times and conditions, listening and watching the sea
I genuinely couldn't stop smiling laughing and generally much more happier
I would sing and do some aerobic dancing while dipping without a care for who would see me.

I have also had some peaceful, private conversations with friends while being buoyant relaxing in the sea.

I've had some great laughs with other sea dippers but also been left alone with my own thoughts while other dippers are there to look out for me while having some alone time
I connected with the sea and Mother Nature.
Not forgetting all the sea minerals and benefit's I

get…sodium, magnesium, sulphur, calcium, potassium, bromine, inorganic carbon, strontium. (To name but a few).

My advice to you, if all the benefits I've mentioned aren't enough, is to be prepared, because once you start wild swimming, you may never stop. You become addicted. Now, I still swim in the local swimming pool and when I swim in the sea, I usually dip with my "Soul Seaster" Lesley. We love to join other local groups if our times fit in with theirs and the groups that we have attended have given a lovely warm welcome.

My sea swimming now, is mostly a little swim around and a few strokes here and there. I never go out my depth, I always wear a swimming aid, and although I have dipped alone I don't recommend it. It's always safer to have someone watch out. HHxx

## Elaine Hardie, 53, Fife

I am a 53 year old married mother of 2 girls. I started swimming outdoors about a year ago when I was on holiday with my husband in Majorca. We hadn't been abroad in years, mainly because I worried about everything, from running out of money to food-poisoning. I watched everyone enjoying the sun, unconcerned about what they looked like in a swimming costume and not afraid of the water at all, and wondered what exactly was holding me back. I got myself a snorkeling mask and joined in. I was surprised how much easier it was to swim in the salty water and had a fantastic time.

When I got home, I started following some local groups on Facebook but still didn't get involved. My youngest daughter has suffered badly from an anxiety disorder which has been adversely affected by the pandemic and we were getting desperate for an improvement. I had read about how icy dips and showers have helped some sufferers improve, so we read the "Ice Man" – Wim Hoff's book which inspired us to try it. Initially we did one minute dips in rivers and the bath at home, which really seemed to help her anxiety, it made her realise she was stronger than she thought she was. When she is struggling now, we get our swimming gear on and get to the nearest beach for a dip.

My first dip with the group in Fife was at 6.30am on the morning of my best friend's funeral. Although I had helped care for her as she battled MND, it was still a shock when it came. I was emotionally drained and felt a bit isolated as all my free time and headspace had been taken up with her suffering and care. I found the group to be welcoming and supportive, offering safety advice, spare equipment and even hugs, without being overly-familiar.

When it comes to the benefits of regular cold-water dips, I feel that I could go on forever! Although I absolutely hate the cold and always have (legend has it I was born with a cardigan on), I feel drawn to the water. I don't find it difficult getting right in, somehow my body is telling me it needs it, like Wim Hoff says "let the body do what the body is capable of doing". It reminds me that my body is a wonderful creation, and is stronger than I realise.
I find being in the water looking out onto the horizon very grounding, it reminds me of my place in the universe, that in perspective my problems are quite small and I need to stop allowing them to become huge in my head.

I also find that my metabolism has changed, I am not as inclined to comfort eat. My energy levels have gone up, especially on the days I am in the water, I feel as if I have had 5 espressos!

I would say to anyone thinking of trying it, to dive right in! You don't need a lot of expensive equipment and a local group will be delighted to guide you. You might find, like me, that your fears and trepidation are quite unfounded, and your super powers will be unleashed!

# Sandra Berry Gove, 66, Leven.

I was first introduced to cold water swimming by my daughter Nicola. She had swam about one year before I ventured into the cold water as an adult. I used to sit and watch her swimming then one day I ventured to the edge of the calm sea and thought I can do this! My first swim was in Pittenweem pool along the East Neuk of Fife. I wore my bathing costume and swim shoes. I have to say it was absolutely freezing lol. I only lasted 5 minutes and my daughter Nicola encouraging me to say positive affirmations. I am strong, I am brave. I am a water heater lol. It was such a brilliant feeling I felt elated.

Since the first swim I bought proper swim shoes and gloves made with Neoprene which I have to say was a game changer. Keeps your feet and hands warm when swimming. Or you can buy a wet suit, I bought one but haven't worn it yet. I quickly learned you need the correct clothes to keep you warm. I bought a swim coat with fur lining or you can buy a swim robe. I also bought joggers and warm woolie socks and hat, these items are a must or just anything warm so you can quickly dry yourself and get changed. All set now to start outdoor swimming seriously and have fun knowing that it is great for your own wellbeing and mental health.

I started swimming outside 2 to 3 times per week and I cannot tell you in words how I felt. It is unbelievable. I felt brave, courageous, strong and great knowing that I had stepped out my comfort zone.

I continued swimming in Pittenweem pool and tried swimming in the sea, here and abroad, not knowing what was in the water, but I knew it was good for me and quickly got over me fear.

I progressed onto doing yoga on the beach, meditation and cold water swimming in the sea which was done in groups of like minded women. I then bought a cold water tub which I sit outside in and I have to say this is fabulous for your mental health and well being sitting outside in the cold water therapy tub listening to the birds or sitting in the rain. It is just so mind blowing bringing in peace to your mind body and soul.

I still do cold water swimming along with swimming in the local pool because the health benefits from cold water therapy are amazing. Improves blood pressure and inflammation, also brilliant for your mental health and makes your brain produce more endorphins – a hormone that makes us feel good and can even relieve pain – to combat the stressful feelings created by the quick change in environment, I would thoroughly recommend Cold water therapy and cold water swimming. Go on take the first step. My friends have joined me and both my daughters both loving the buzz!

Love and light, Sandra Berry Gove

# Karen Lindley, Nottingham

Why I like cold water swimming.

There is something that keeps me going back for more-a combination of the mental challenge of getting in, the exhilaration of the cold prickling on my body-I feel alive and present in the moment, the calmness of quietly and gently swimming at my own pace in a beautiful unspoilt spot, with plenty of room, no one disturbing me, or racing by splashing me with their wind milling crawl. Just a few ducks, and geese sharing their space.

I enjoy the fresh air smell, the cleanness of the water. The lack of chemicals. The cold takes away my joint pain, the aching muscles from the weightlifting sessions I also enjoy, and the constant itching I experience from eczema. It calms the chatter in my mind as I focus on swimming, monitoring the cold, enjoying watching my hands stretching out in the clean cold water.

I enjoy the camaraderie of the group I swim with-the support-some people swim in a group-I call them the flotilla-I swim by myself, but I do like to keep an eye on their colourful tow floats bobbing along, knowing that I am not completely alone. I like to join the communal café table after my swim for a coffee and cake, and sit in the sun, warming myself up, cosily wrapped in nothing but my changing robe, feeling that all is right in my world.

I like to measure my stats and notice that my swimming has improved, and I have got faster, my asthmatic breathing is even more under control. I'm interested in the health benefits, especially the brown fat activation. I feel myself to be calmer, more composed, less likely to get riled by day-to-day trivialities (that must be the dopamine). I like to journal my swims, and reflect on what I achieved, what the weather was like, what was different, what wildlife I saw.

I like swimming on a balmy August evening, when the cold water seems to wash away the stresses of the day, I like swimming at night, under the full moon, when everyone is decked out in pretty coloured lights, I like swimming in the rain, and on a quiet misty morning when you can hardly see anyone else, and I feel like have the whole lake to myself. This will be my first full winter swimming season, and I'm looking forward to it with a little trepidation, and a lot of anticipation.

I've always enjoyed a dip in very cold water- ever since I used to go to Harrogate Turkish baths as a teenager and loved the cold plunge pool. I can't resist a dip in the sea, especially if the sun is shining and the water looks all sparkly.

I have found that it helps to find a venue that is close by as driving a long way home afterwards can be difficult if you are very cold. Keep your swim bag ready packed with all the necessary bits, towelling changing robe, slides, lights tow float, gloves, neoprene socks, woolly hat, cossie and then you are ready to go and won't put it off instead, or leave it too late to go, dithering around packing. Arrange to meet up with a like-minded swim buddy for your first few swims.

Know that there is nothing wrong with being a bit scared. That is what will keep you safe. Read lots of books about the benefits of cold-water swimming, they are very inspiring and will encourage you in your own attempts at becoming a cold-water swimmer.

Swimming with Whole Health

## Lynne Waddle, 54, West Lothian

Cold water therapy or wild swimming as others call it certainly isn't for everyone but don't knock it till you've tried it at least once.

I started swimming outdoors just before the start of the pandemic mainly because I had heard about the benefits and had seen lots of posts on social media of how much fun it could be. I started swimming once a week at first then a couple of times a week after kitting myself out with all the gear, after this I dipped in and out of swimming (no pun intended). Now I swim with 3 or 4 others on a regular basis spending varied amounts of time in the water.

It's a great way to meet friends, get outside and just to put all the days worries aside for a little while, at the moment not swimming as much because our wee tribe like a wee bit of heat in the water so taking a little break. Looking forward to the lighter nights and the weather being a bit warmer to start swimming again.

If you've never tried it before be brave and try it, who knows you may just like it. What better way is there to meet friends old and new.

## You

What or who are you giving your attention to?
I hope it's you.
I hope it's you who you're channeling energy to.
You and not the who.
Or what.
If not.
Then do.
Do who you are.
Love who you are.
It's important and you're worth the effort.
Stay faithful to you.

LjG

# Isabel Traynor, 55, Leslie, Fife, Scotland

I have a very stressful job and over the last four years I have had so many breakdowns. I have learned mindfulness I have an app on my phone feeling good and I have had professional counselling. I have found them all helpful but still something was missing. I saw Laurie's post on the Fife Floaters page for a wee dip at loch ore and was so excited. I had been watching and thinking about wild swimming. I came along and had a wonderful time and the feeling of completeness has been what I've had missing in my life. I so look forward to our swims it puts my body and mind back into alignment.

Most importantly I have met wonderful people and made new friends I cherish every moment and every swim cause it makes me able to cope with whatever life chooses to throw at me next.

# Louise Lawson, 56, Dundee

Why do I swim outdoors?

This is something I have been thinking about lately, initially it was a bit of green-eyed monster and Fear of missing out. To explain that statement, pre covid I used to dance a lot. The style was Fusion Bellydance, I attended classes, danced at outdoor events, on the stage and was part of the charity Confidance for Life, we were our own little community. As with so many other things it all kind of ground to a halt.

When I discovered that one of my fellow dancers was now wild swimming I wanted in, I wanted to feel that I was doing something again, I had been inactive for so long that my body had gotten so much larger. I was envious of her courage to go in the water, to be seen in swimming gear. I guess my reasoning behind my decision was not really the right one, I had not really thought about swimming that much until my friend did it.

My first attempt in March lasted about a min or two, there were lots of "oh dear lords" escaping my mouth and then a "nope not happening" as it was so cold, you should see the video of shrieks lol. Something must have stuck though as I went back with her to do it again. When we go somewhere for a swim, I really enjoy the banter with the people I swim with, everyone is so friendly and welcoming to us.
We don't have a specific beach that we go to, we tend to travel around trying different swimming places. This gives us not only the opportunity to see the countryside and the coast, but also to meet a wider amount of people. There are people from all walks of life swimming now, everyone

swimming for their own reasons, all of them for a better reason than why I started I suspect. The swimmers are also all shapes and sizes, and no one judges you. In fact, quite a few have recommended places to get large size swimming gear, which I am most grateful for.

I am very self-conscious about my body, I hate having such large boobs, even when dancing there was always a bit of me that thought I was being judged for my size. What I have found with swimming though, is that I don't mind if people see me with wet clothes sticking to my larger body, I feel good that I have the courage to go into the cold water, where so many others don't.

Swimming makes me happy and calm. If I feel stressed at work, I just want to get in the water. I think my favourite swim at the moment is Loch Cluny, there is something about the stillness of the water, surrounded by trees and hills, and the sun reflecting on the water that sooths my soul. I have an underactive thyroid so tend to feel the cold a lot, this is making me think I will swim less during this season.

However, to keep myself active and get into a better state of fitness, I have now signed up for a Pilates class and a stretch class to keep me motivated over the winter. If I had not gone swimming, I never would have plucked up the courage to go and do other activities.

I would like to end this by saying thank you so much to Karen for letting me join you wild swimming, I feel alive again.

Tahlulla x

# Sandy Toms-Mann, 37, Hertfordshire

I was at my most successful during secondary school. I had an identity, I had a sense of Self. This deteriorated slightly during 6th form, returned for a shining first year of university, and then pretty much vanished into the abyss from my second year onwards.

In this fog of non-identity, I married and had two beautiful, wonderful little boys. I developed a sort of identity, but it was very much as O and M's mother rather than an identity of my own.

I wasn't really doing any of things I had previously enjoyed so much and whilst I loved (and still love) being a mum, I didn't know who I was anymore - I didn't recognise myself at all.

Fast-forward some years: a divorce, single parenting, a variety of jobs, a new husband, and five house-moves, and I found myself barely clinging on to the proverbial life raft with the occasional thunderous waves crashing over my already-soaked head.

"You need to find something for yourself." My step-mum said to me a couple of months ago. "Something that will help you meet new people, get back to being a bit more You." (I am a complete introvert and would rather be in bed by 8pm that out socialising.

I said that I always feel a pull towards the water and love swimming, but the sea is so far away. "Why don't you try wild swimming?" I thought that sounded rather good.

(Whenever my husband and I are near a body of water we will almost certainly swim in it, even if it means going in in our underwear and travelling home wet), so why this never occurred to me I don't know!) Within the hour she sent me some links to some Facebook groups. I immediately signed up to Facebook and joined a selection of said groups.

Less than a week later found me on my own at Westthorpe Lake at 7.30 in the morning. I was physically shaking with nerves as I approached the desk to pay and find out how the whole craziness worked. The guy was, of course, lovely, kind and helpful. There was a decent number of people there and the buzz and atmosphere was something completely new to me.

I just did two rounds of the 400m loop but you know what? I could have stayed in all day. I felt free. I felt light. I felt completely content and happy. The high I had from this swim lasted me three and a half days. I was hooked.

I have swum every weekend since then. The high lasts me until about Wednesday and then I'm excited about the coming weekend and swimming again. If I can squeeze in extra swims (or even just a dip) I will. It has been amazing to rope my husband, brother and two boys into it (they're only 9 and 11 - never too young to start!) and none of us can get enough of it.

The organised swims such as full moon swims are well attended and, like my first swim, the atmosphere is fabulous. There is something utterly magical about swimming under a full moon with little neon tow floats bobbing around, or in a torrential rain fall where the sight, sound and feel of the rain is like nothing else.

If you're on the edge, if you're unsure, if you're not sold yet - do it. Just take the plunge (pun very much intended). You won't look back. And if the winter-cold water isn't for you, it's just as glorious when it's warm too. It doesn't have to be about braving the winter ice! Just go for it. GO FOR IT! It is epic. I completely come alive when I swim and ridiculously animated when I talk to people about it.

All your problems melt away. They are forgotten. They don't matter. They don't exist. For a blissful, magical chunk of time, you will feel free and content. And this lovely feeling sticks around!

I feel like I am rapidly coming to back to myself. To an identity that is mine and mine alone. I love it and could not rate it any more highly.

Oh, and also - if you like Stuff like me, there's a brilliant selection of things to buy! Also, it is very often free to swim, which is always an excellent bonus.

# Kreisha Szaranek, 48 years old, Glenrothes, Fife

I began swimming after Covid after my mental health took a dive. Although I have always suffered with my mental health, after Covid and being in lockdown on my own, with my 2.5 year old daughter, my anxiety went through the roof. I began to struggle with social settings and even going to a shop for example.

After seeing some posts on Facebook, I decided to give it a try. I'd heard about the benefits and was intrigued. I didn't buy any gear to begin with as I wanted to see how I went first. I was lucky enough to come across a swimming group quite local to me and arranged to meet up with someone who was from the same area as me. I'm not the strongest of swimmers (and always like my feet to be touching the bottom) but she assured me she was the same and we'd go at my pace.

When arriving I was really nervous. The lady I met was amazing and very patient, and really helped me feel at ease, especially when wading in and the water began to get quite cold – despite it being summer. As soon as I got in and bobbed about on my (borrowed) tow float, I was hooked. The feeling of being submerged in the water was something I'd never experienced before. It was amazing.

Since then (2020) I have been swimming as frequently as possible. Unfortunately, this isn't as often as I'd like but I go as often as I can. If I lived closer to the sea I'd be in daily that's for sure.

If you're thinking about it, STOP! Just do it, Not only is the benefits great for so much more than your mental health, there's the physical benefits also. The social aspect of it is also amazing, There's the sense of belonging. The friendships formed. The check-ins from others when they know you have things going on in their personal lives. The big dooks, the tour of Scotland for different locations. Swimming has it all. Do it, you won't be disappointed.

# Linda-Lou, 50, Kirkcaldy

The start of my Wild Swimming Journey, where it came from.

After many years of going through a mentally challenging time (2 mental and abusive partners leading to relationship breakdowns and that's just the shortened version) not to mention bringing up my 2 boys (whom I love dearly) on my own, then before you know it BOOM! The menopause hits! It was time for a radical change in my life, starting with hypnosis sessions on finding myself again and overcoming past traumas. All of which worked great. But there was still something missing.

Then, as I was walking along Kingsbarns Beach on a very cold February Sunday, I stood looking at the sea and thought "I want to go in". So I did. I just rolled up my leggings to my thighs, no socks or shoes and just went in with my bare feet. I stood there with my eyes closed embracing the sea, the air and the cold, taking in all the surroundings. The only way I could describe it was I was walking into something that felt natural and at home to me. I felt it was like where I belonged. Also my star sign is Aquarius and my zodiac symbol is a water barer. So I think that totally resonates with me and the water. I felt so alive and I've never looked back since!

After mentioning it to my friend Lynn she said both her and her daughter Chloe fancied the cold water too, and so, one week later we were all in at Pathhead Sands for our first full cold swim. The next week The Bonnie Black Swans were formed. That was 3 years ago.

Mentally and physically the cold water therapy works wonders for me. My menopause symptoms have been much easier to manage, and the difference in my mental health has helped tenfold. My life has to include cold water therapy on a weekly basis. I make a point of swimming being in my diary weekly, the colder the better for me. LOVE IT. And to you I say. Be bold, be brave and let the cold water therapy embrace your mind and body.

# Sarah Griffiths, 49, Cheshire

Finding Solace and Resilience Through Wild and Cold-Water Swimming.

As a woman of a certain age, approaching 50 with hormones going crazy and life even crazier… my world, like many others' is full of stress. We all have responsibilities as employees, home keepers, parents, carers, friends, and well, just survivors in a life filled with more stress and responsibilities. My journey is, I suppose a quest for serenity and renewal amidst the chaos of life, that I didn't realise I was looking for.

The last few years have been exceptionally traumatic to say the least. I work in public health, so work has been even more demanding than usual since 2020, for obvious reasons, but in addition to the home and work stress that the pandemic brought I ended up dealing with emotional stress and trauma like I've never experienced before.

My gorgeous dad, the stable, the solid, the quietly loving and uber supportive person in my life died suddenly in early 2020, and then just weeks later my mum had an accident and broke her pelvis. Just at the point that the world was beginning to change and shut down.
It was a whirlwind of a few weeks running from and to their house (they lived 30 miles away) the hospital, undertakers, solicitors etc and I can hardly remember now a single moment of it. But in mid-March, the date my mum was released early from hospital (still incapacitated but because wards were filling up) I became very suddenly unwell and ended up being blue lighted to hospital with some form of

cardiac or lung event. I was in hospital when the world closed, when my children couldn't go to school, and when no one could visit.

Everyone had to manage on their own. Eventually though and it would be many months before I was diagnosed, I was told I had 'Broken Heart Syndrome' – which just rocked my world. I also didn't realise until some time after when I was even struggling to manage everyday things without falling apart, that I was suffering with PTSD as a result of everything.

This is the story of how I discovered a path to solace and tranquillity in an unexpected place – wild and cold-water swimming.

I, self-admittedly, could very well have been "the coldest person in the world," given my aversion to cold weather. Watching some of the Wim Hof bits on TV and hearing some testimony kindled a spark of wonderment, the idea of this intriguing therapy piqued my curiosity, and I couldn't help but wonder if it might 'do something for me'.
By some random coincidence, I stumbled on some posts on Facebook from a school gate mum, who I only vaguely knew, with pictures of swim wear and woolly hats in March! Inspired by their courage, or stupidity I contacted them out of the blue and mustered the bravery to join their ranks. Little did I know that this leap of faith would become a profound turning point in my life.

From the very first day, when I tagged along just for the fun of it... I was hooked. The release and the joy I felt when plunging into the chilly natural world were indescribable. It was an instant hit, I noticed how literally the noise of my mind stilled instantly, closed off, shut down and focussed on nothing at all other than just being, just breathing, concentrating on the sensations of my body. I achieved a level of mindfulness that no end of self-help books, meditation, sound baths, howling in woods has ever been able to achieve!

That was it, I then seemed to be attending our 'local lake' (it takes a good 40 minutes to get there) and local accessible coastline as often as I could. Appreciating the 'hit' every time, just like the first. I began to notice and enjoy the changing scenery, the evolving environment through different seasons and hours of the day that Id previously have wasted slumbering in bed or vegetating in front of the TV – it all held me spellbound. Wild swimming quickly became more than a hobby; it was a source of profound peace and tranquillity.

The appeal of cold-water swimming extended beyond the picturesque surroundings. It demanded mindfulness, pushing me to be present in the most genuine way. Submerging myself in icy waters, I had to focus on each breath, find the rhythm of my heart, and stay afloat. In those moments, I discovered the therapeutic power of being in harmony with myself.

The first year was marked by unwavering dedication. No matter the weather or the season, I would venture into the lake, wearing nothing more than a swimming costume, gloves, and boots. One unforgettable morning saw me, and the group of equally bonkers ladies arrive at the lake with an axe in case it was needed to break through the ice – we failed to break through but the laughs, the friendship, the oneness and belonging was equally as beneficial as the chilly mindfulness. Each challenge, faced with my newfound 'tribe' only made me stronger, more resilient, and better equipped to face the complexities of life.

My life continues to be fraught with stress. My job remains demanding, and the responsibilities of caring for my mum have only increased with a diagnosis of Alzheimer's. Yet, my newfound love for cold water swimming had given me an inner strength I never knew I possessed.
The friendships I formed with my fellow swimmers, bound by a shared devotion to the extraordinary and an acceptance of each other's quirks, became an essential source of support. Together, we found solace in laughter, even in the most challenging and absurd situations. This tight-knit community, connected by our love for cold water, pursuit of peace and never wavered in commitment.

For me, cold water swimming had transformed into a sacred ritual. It became my daily medication, a remedy for both my physical and mental well-being. It offered me an escape from the burdens of everyday life and allowed me to find moments of pure joy and contentment.

My journey from trauma and stress to peace and resilience was a deeply personal one. Cold water swimming became my sanctuary, a place where I could temporarily shed the worries of life and nurture a renewed spirit. My story is a testament to the remarkable healing power of nature and the strength that can be found within a community of like-minded individuals. Cold water swimming is more than just a hobby for me; it is a way of life, a lifeline, and a tribute to the indomitable human spirit.

## Josie McMaster, 51, West Yorkshire

I had an early menopause in my late thirties brought on, I believe, by emotional trauma. As my menopause symptoms were manageable with Black Cohosh, I did not pursue any other treatment. With hindsight, I may have done. Over the years I have developed joint pains that never really go away. Blood tests reveal nothing significant, so I look for alternative therapies, where I find the practitioners are genuinely baffled by the extent of my knotted-up muscles. The most recent Osteopath suggested swimming to loosen up my upper back and shoulders. My husband wanted to try Outdoor Swimming. I didn't particularly fancy it but couldn't find any enthusiasm for battling it out in a crowded swimming baths either.

Around this time someone was offering an Induction to Outdoor Swimming at a private lake not far from where I live. It promised beautiful moorland scenery, wildlife and cake, so ignoring my significant reservations I signed up.

Despite what I thought was meticulous planning, I arrived late, and wondered if I should read the signs and accept it wasn't for me, but still I felt compelled to try it. I remained trepidatious throughout the introductory talk and latched onto the advice "just focus on your breathing". The scenery was beautiful, the lake was brown and there was a lot of mud to wade through before it was deep enough to swim, but oh my goodness, within minutes I was addicted.

I had to keep doing this, so I searched the internet and found a group who swim close by and throughout the summer I joined someone for a swim most mornings. I started outdoor swimming because I was looking for physical respite, and I found it. It is not a cure, but I take a lot less pain relief than I did. What I had not anticipated was the impact on my mental health and more general wellbeing. It is difficult to summarise the experience of swimming in cold water surrounded by nature, either taking it in quietly alone or using the opportunity to get to know the like-minded people around you.

Maybe if I had to select a salient point, it is the sensation shortly after the shock of the cold water subsides when I start to feel a sort of mental clearing, and everything I was worrying about loses its significance. With the exception of that moment in the water, everything loses its significance, and some sort of comfortable perspective is possible. And then there is the post-swim buzz, which lasts long enough to give you time to book yourself onto your next swim. I am now looking at my first winter of Outdoor Swimming and I plan to stick with it. To anyone thinking about it, I would say find your local group, contact them and try it. Whatever your reservations are, something has drawn you to it and, for me, it has been somehow life-changing.

# Cristina Wilkie, 54, Perthshire

Approximately 3 years ago I was talking to a facilitator at Mindspace (mental health charity). She was sounding me out for a new 6 weeks course she was considering on 'open water swimming' at Willowgate Activity Centre. This was in Feb/Mar – I joked maybe if you thought about it in June or July, I might consider it then – well blow me it started at the end of June on a Thursday evening so I really felt I couldn't say no! What a brilliant experience though, with a great group and when we were asked to guess the temperature etc. We were more often wrong than right. A massive surprise to me considering my legs were like jelly when I came out of the water but they've definitely strengthened up a lot since then.

I really got a bug for it as it happens and there are only 2 from the group who go at least once a week – generally on a Sunday morning! It is such a great opportunity to get hints and tips or support new people. We are now part of a mad group of 6-8 ladies (aged from 30-60) who encouraged each other (including participating in themed swims), have a very close bond & look out for each other (even not on swim days). After our swim we often go to the cafe, where we enjoy breakfast and further chat/laughter – with our partners too. The staff look forward to our visits and look after us. This year we have ventured out which has been lovely – Elie, Aberdour, Leven & Loch Venacher. Picnics on the beach.

My family and some friends think I am nuts but as my dad has rheumatoid arthritis, he understands these things are beneficial for your mental and physical health so they're delighted I have found something that gives me pleasure – to be honest I still question what I get from my swims – I know for sure that the humidity in a swimming pool is not good for me and the pleasure of being outdoors with amazing scenery, with like-minded people is. Experiencing all seasons and I can honestly say my favourite time is winter for the ice – it's the weirdest experience but the most memorable!

Almost 10 years ago I was diagnosed with MS, my mobility is affected along with various other symptoms. Sadly, stress is a major trigger for me – I've been married to Ian for 33 years and we've experienced some challenges over the years – especially this year! I honestly think if I didn't live with this debilitating condition, I would never have considered it but I love surprising people & there's more to come before the year is out!

I would encourage you to give it a go, you've got nothing to lose & don't worry what you look like, that's not important, it is what you get out of your dip/swim. There are lots of group, get chatting it's a lovely community. Many people enjoy it for health reasons or just because they enjoy swimming al fresco – just ensure you don't overdo it and definitely don't do it alone (even if your partner just observes you).

# Nicky Foulds, 47, Cornwall

I cannot remember a time when I haven't swum, other than when my leg was in plaster following a ski accident. Having been born and raised in Cornwall, my sister and I were taught to swim as kids and spent many happy times on the beach and in rivers and pools on the moors. Fast forward to adulthood (very overrated!), moving to London, pursuing a career, getting married then full circle back, I wanted my children to have the same happy outdoorsy childhood so here I am back swimming in the same waters and feeling very blessed to be able to do so. The fact that 97% of the earth's water is ocean and the ancient mariner's saying "water water everywhere and not a drop to drink" implies that we are surrounded by a resource we cannot benefit from, we actually can, by being in it.

An increasing number of people are discovering not just the physical, but the mental benefits of open water swimming. We already know that exercise, fresh air and social interaction are all good for us, but there is science-based evidence to prove that a cold water swim focusses the mind as the numerous books, papers and studies on the subject illustrate. As a regular sea swimmer, I can vouch for the fact that it is good for mental and physical health and I keep getting back in the water to preserve mine.

These days more dipping and chatting goes on than head down swimming, but the wetsuit still goes on for a couple of km if the conditions are good and there are many charity swims and events for swimmers of all levels.

My personal highlight was the Scilly Swim Challenge, a

15km swim and walk around the islands, you don't get better than a sunny Scilly day. Of course, being the UK that isn't always the case, but whatever the weather getting in the water is addictive, whether it's the adrenaline rush, the naturally increased dopamine levels or simply the fresh air and getting away from it all.

The sea is a sanctuary, gives solace and can provide the perfect reset. Not everyone swims for these reasons, some sea and lake swimmers are competitive athletes, contemplative dippers or simply enjoy the feeling of being in the water and/or the social interaction – all valid reasons, everyone is different and it's all ok. The open water swimming community is vast, with many online and local swimming groups welcoming people from all backgrounds and abilities all with a common interest. Where the actual water is concerned, some prefer it salty, some fresh, but its salty sea and sand in your toes all the way for me. Many lasting friendships come from where we least expect them with swim buddies helping each other through the ups and downs of life – what is discussed in the waves stays in the waves! Some have made their living from their love of open water swimming, from providing guided swims, swim camps and training to writing inspiring books such as this one.

My local swim spot of Bude Sea Pool is an iconic man made 91m long tidal pool, managed with membership monies, maintained by volunteers and free to all. We are blessed with numerous beaches, with the north coast of Cornwall being more wild and rugged and the south coast calmer. That's not to say we don't get some flat conditions, it's abandon everything and head to the sea when the Surfline app shows 0-1 ft waves

As I write, in early November just after Storm Ciarán it is showing 10-15 feet so maybe safety should prevail. Which is another important factor; always be aware of conditions and weather forecasts, tell someone where you are swimming and my personal advice would be never swim alone, but many do and I myself have been known to take an impromptu skinny dip! The most important thing is to listen to your body, especially in the winter.

Afterdrop is a very real thing and can be dangerous and although that post swim tingle is a great feeling, the cooled blood soon starts to circulate again so get dressed and warm quickly. Anyone taking their first dip is encouraged to do it in the Summer or Autumn and acclimatise through the winter, it is said that a general rule of thumb is 1 minute per degree but the "touch each finger with your thumb" method always works for me, though the shivers still set in sometimes. The bottom line is getting in that water and jumping in the waves makes you feel like a kid again and we could all do with some of that.

I mostly swim with the same group of people, who have become a huge part of my life, one is my sister so we have followed our swim journey together. We have our sacred swim week on Scilly every September and regularly meet to swim, though sometimes if conditions aren't good, we just sit in our vans and put the world to rights.

As mentioned there are numerous swim groups around, but the ones I am involved with are BOWS (Bude Open Water Swimmers), North Cornwall OWLS (Open Water Leisure Swimmers), Cornwall Sea Swimmers, WASPS (Walk and Swim Porthpean), Cornwall Wild Swimming and Ocean City Swimmers. Just thinking of all the lovely, inspirational people I have met through these groups makes me smile. There is also the hugely successful worldwide Bluetits group, details of these and others can all be found on Facebook.

Finally, if you are thinking of taking a dip, don't be put off by the mention of distance or depth, don't worry about ability, shape or size, just find a swim buddy or local swim group and go for it! Leave your worries on the shoreline and you will never regret a swim.

In the words of Van Morrison "smell the sea and feel the sky, let your soul and spirit fly"

# Julia McFall, 52, London.

I have swum for most of my life. Mostly in pools. Mostly alone. Reasonably well but not in a get up at 5am and train before school kind of way. In my 20s and early 30s I'd crack off 100 lengths before work and was generally pretty fit.

Relationships came, relationships went. After another 'you're not quite right' relationship bit the dust, I found myself in Canada at the wedding of a friend. But a small wedding held in a house on a private lake where the guests stayed for a week and swam and canoed on the lake and beyond. Freshwater swimming was a revelation – no sand, no waves, just a limpid intensity. Feeling fairly forlorn on the wedding night itself, the groom's mother's suggestion that we slip off and swim in the dark was welcome. We left our clothes at the water's edge and skinny dipped. It was the most magical swim of my life.

Fast forward 15 years, and now living in East London, an unremarkable suburban life. On the micro-level a busy professional job, two kids (with a strong neurospicy streak), a significant community voluntary role, an elderly parent and a sibling fighting a prolonged battle with Motor Neurone Disease.

On a macro level, all sorts of existential despair about the State of the World. Constant fire-fighting, calendar juggling (and failing!), head whizz and insomnia, anger, insecurity and guilt whirling - and a bit of menopause action as the icing on the cake. Exercise had long been displaced by "other things I had to do". Luckily in our part of East London there are a lot of parks, flats and forests and long family walks were the order of the day. There are also a lot of lakes and without fail on every walk I would say to my husband "wouldn't it be amazing if we could swim here".

And then one day we could. We had to pay, we had to be inducted and we can only go at certain times, but there is a gem of a lake only ten minutes from my house. I have been going every Saturday morning since for two years. It is the most selfish thing I have done since being a parent. I started going with a friend. We went to try it. We set no expectations. No "we must do this three times a week or we will have failed". We went because we wanted to. We loved it, and we went back. A weekly water worship, a confessional and a washing away of sins.

When you step into the cold water you cannot think of anything else but how you feel. As you get deeper and approach full immersion everything else is gone. The noise in your head is silenced by the overwhelming rush of cold. Often you swear and then you start to laugh. A glorious, releasing laugh at the ridiculousness of what you are doing. You wait for your friend or she waits for you and then you start swimming, trying to remember to breathe slowly to help the cold panic of your body settle. And then it does and you can swim, remarkably, even in very low temperatures.

We are confined to laps, the first one we usually chat round, processing each other's weeks and the second a more solitary head-in -the-water swim, sometimes pushing ourselves, sometimes not, the free-ing thing being the complete lack of expectation. And when we have had enough we get out – and begin the much more physically challenging task of getting changed in the cold.

For me the feeling of being out in the middle of a deep lake on a bright winter's day is like no other. It is uplifting and elemental. It is rationalising and grounding and deeply personal. I honestly believe it has kept me (relatively) sane over the last couple of years. If you're thinking about trying it, do. There is nothing to lose and everything to gain.

A word also on community and kit.

The lake community is so friendly and non-judgemental, this kind of swimming is a broad church of folk where some people are pursuing serious athletic goals and the rest of us are just enjoying the swim, but I have never felt any pressure to do more. And as to kit, you can get some but you don't need a lot, and I've just added to it bit by bit. I swim in a wetsuit in the winter because I want to stay in the water as long as possible, and I have gloves and boots. These have proved very worthy investments. There are a few nice-to-haves – fleecy changing robes etc, but they are not necessary.

Don't let lack of kit put you off!

# By the Light of the Silvery Moon

Sunset and Sunrise Swimming really are magical – and the photos are epic when you catch a decent one. That orange egg yolk suns against the silky blue hues of the sky and the sea are incredible and nothing will beat the silhouette of a dipper walking into the sea with a sunrise in the background. It is just the stuff that dreams are made of. But did you know, there is an even more magical time, just before and just after a sunrise? That is the golden hour and the blue hour.

The terms 'golden hour' and 'blue hour' are often referred to for sunset and sunrise swims. The terms can be deceptive because they rarely last a full hour. Sometimes, they can be as little as 15 minutes, but they really are beautiful if you catch at them right time. So, here's a wee explanation of both;

Golden hour occurs just after sunrise and just before sunset, when the sun is low in the sky but sitting just above the horizon. Golden hour creates a warm and fuzzy feeling, kissing everything it reaches in gold. A bit like the Midas touch.

Blue hour occurs a little before sunrise and a little after the sun has set just below the horizon, this produces those cooler blue tones, making everything appear silvery, mysterious, darker and somewhat colder.

Swimming at any of these times feels incredibly magical and are usually the quietest of times which are both my personal favourites. I couldn't choose between them, but either way you will have some truly special photos and memories. My first dook was during both golden and blue hour. It really was magical.

Swimming Under a Full Moon is something special too. Another magical time to be in the water, especially when the diamond like reflections of the moonlight dance and glisten on the ripples and waves. It creates your very own disco dance floor and it feels quite magical.
Dancing in the moonlight but in the sea.

All Moons are great for swimming though and it's great to have a basic understanding of the Moons cycle, not just for our own "monthly" happenings but for the tides too.

Each tide is very different to the one before and brings with it so much more momentum depending on times of high tides and low tides. The full moon and new moon also play havoc with those tides as do the Spring and Autumn Equinox. So here are some more basics for you, without too much of the jargon.

I've tried to keep these explanations as simple as possible, so if you're looking for a more in depth "lesson" this is not the book for you. This is just a brief description of tides and currents, there are other books out there and lots of information online that will go into more detail. For now though, here are "the basics" that you need to know. I've also included a few "magical" tips for you to do around these times too.

# Understanding Tides and Dangers

Spring tides (full moon, new moon)

When the moon is full in the sky (whether visible in a clear sky or hidden behind clouds) the high tide will be a higher tide than normal. That means it will be deeper water and there will be a stronger pull/current. The same goes for the new moon, which falls 2 weeks after a full moon. On a new moon, the high tide will be high as well. During a full and new moon, the low tide will be much lower and shallow. Where I swim, the water on a low tide during a full moon is usually a good walk from the shore, however on a high tide, we can almost step in right away.

Neap tide (first and third quarter moon – the times between the new moon and full moon)

On neap tides, the swells are the opposite of those on a full and new moon. This means that the high tides are lower/shallower and low tides are higher/fuller than they are on a spring tides, meaning less water is moving, occurring every two weeks one week after a full moon and new moon.

The actual heights and intervals of tides vary completely depending on location so it is important to know the tides of the area you are going to. Having this information will aid you in making a more informed choice for a swimming spot!

Flooding and Ebbing tide

The rising of the tide is known as a flooding tide (tide coming in) and an ebbing tide is also known as a falling tide (tide going out).

When the tide is out fully, potential hazards are exposed on the sea bed, revealing rocks and other risks that may cause rip tides. A falling tide or a low tide are the perfect time to do your beach combing if you like to search for treasures.

When the tide is in fully, hazards are hidden, so its advised that when swimming somewhere new to investigate the terrain on a low tide first. Equally, if there's been storms and strong winds, you're always safer checking out the damage on a low tide.

Slack tides

This is the brief time after a high or low tide when the water has the least movement and is just about to switch again from flooding (water coming in/tide rising) to ebbing (water going out/tide falling). The opposite is a low slack, the tide has gone all the way down and the current comes to a brief stop as it switches from ebbing to flooding.

Rip Currents

Rip currents are usually formed when there is a build-up of water on the beach from the tide and waves. This build up will flow from the shoreline back out to sea and can carry you out and away at the same time. They are strong and can be dangerous.

A rip current can be split into 3 parts. The first being the feeder current which is where it starts, hence "feeder". This is where the water is building up along the shoreline. This water runs parallel to the sea until it finds the easiest path back out to sea. Then there is the neck. This is the easiest path for the water to flow back out to sea and is usually formed by a carved out shape in the sand/seabed. The current is strong at this point and this is where you will feel the biggest pull from the water. The head of a rip current is where the build-up water discharges back into the sea.

There are so many things to look out for when trying to spot a rip current, but the most important thing is that there is often a lack of waves in an area where there are lots of waves breaking around about. People often mistake this calm spot in the water as a safe area to enter. Sometimes however, you can't see them at all and they are so quick to appear out of nowhere. So understanding a little about them is important if you're going to be spending your spare time in the water.

So, how do you get out of a rip current if you are caught out? Well, the first thing to remember is to not panic. Panicking burns energy and you want to save as much of that as you possibly can, you might in this situation for some time before either rescued or released and this can be exhausting if you try to fight against it. Key thing to remember is to float. Put your head back and spread your arms, allow the current to carry you. If you can, try and swim adjacent to the shore and not directly towards the shore. Instinctively you will want to swim toward the beach again, but you can never swim out of a rip current that way. Stay calm, raise one arm and wave to someone signaling for help.

The weather can also play a major part in how the water behaves, for various reasons, but I don't want to overload you with too much information on this. If it is something you want to look into more, there are plenty websites out there that will give all the information you need to know especially when it comes to offshore winds and storms etc.

There have been a few storms recently which have affected the surface and debris at our regular swim spot and even though the storms have now passed, the beach is still changing daily and on a high tide, the risk of rip tides is much higher now.

Checking your location is so important, especially if its somewhere new, but as I said even our regular beach changes daily, with new risks appearing every tide, we have to keep an regular watch to make sure we don't get caught out and we always swim with a buddy, even if they are just "spotting" for you from the shore.

# Staying Safe

Things to look out for

Apart from the currents and weather, there are many other risks to take into account and be on the look out for such as jellyfish and other aquatic creatures. On our coast in Scotland, there are often reports of seals, dolphins, whales and even sharks and although thankfully, not as common as other locations around the world, we still need to keep a watchful eye.

As mentioned before, always check out the area and do your research before swimming somewhere new. In fact before swimming in general, you should always scope the (land)scape.

Afterdrop

This is when your body continues to cool down after you have left the water. It can happen to any one of us and even the most seasoned swimmer can experience the phenomenon. It's nothing to be ashamed of or embarrassed about. The key thing to help move through this or to try and prevent it from happening is to always have a hot drink after your swims. It's a great way to help heat up your core and you get to have a blether with your buddies. I always have hot water bottle as well and lots of warm clothes to layer up.

Cold Water Shock

Cold water shock can happen to anyone as well. This is when we have entered the water too quickly and our body has not had enough time to regulate properly. This can easily be avoided though, by concentrating on your breathing and observing your body's reactions. Remember, everyone is different, it's not a race to see who gets in first.

Offshore vs Onshore wind

Offshore wind is the most dangerous type of wind as depending on how strong it is, you can be blown out to sea. Offshore winds blow directly off the beach and out to sea.

Onshore wind blows towards land so is the opposite to offshore wind, however, an onshore wind can cause waves which in themselves could be dangerous! Look out for those white horses! Unless, like me, you love jumping waves.

Cross shore is probably quite self-explanatory and is when the wind blows either from left to right or right to left along the shore. This wind can also be quite treacherous if underestimated and you should always look out for the ninja waves (the ones that appear out of nowhere).

I personally love jumping around in the waves because the feeling as they crash against you is indescribable. I am instantly transported to 6 year old me playing at the beach with my cousins. Nothing else matters.

# Moon Magic and Simple Sea Rituals

The moon as I explained earlier has a gravitational influence on our tides and the cycle of the moon (29.5 days) can also help women tune into their own monthly cycle. In other cultures, the moon is a symbol of change and growth, learning and letting go. These are also often connected to the stages of the Moons cycle with the waning moon being the time for letting go, surrendering, releasing, and silence. This phase is the period after a full moon before a new moon. The moon is visibly decreasing and releasing.

A new moon on the other hand opens us up to the possibility of new beginnings. It's the time to start afresh. This is the time when the moon is dark in the sky and unseen. It encourages us to take a leap of faith and plant the seeds for the coming weeks.

With a waxing moon, we see growth, manifestation and making wishes. It represents the positive growth in people and is the time just after a new moon, where it reappears in the sky and is growing into our beautiful full moon which represents the point of success and achievement. If you have planted the metaphorical seeds during the new moon and they have not yet come to fruition, the waning full moon following your new moon is the perfect time to let go of the energy that could be blocking your success.

At any of these moon phases it is great to stand at the waters edge and cast you wishes in to the depths of the sea. Visualisation can be so powerful. So, when looking to release and let go, write in the sand, "that thing" you want to set free.

Allow the waves to wash it away and visualise it clearing out from your soul with every wave that arrives.

Likewise on a new moon and when planting new seeds of hope, a lovely ritual to perform is to search the beach for a shell that represents what you would like to manifest. Stand at the waters edge, visualise your seeds in the shell being carried off across the world to grow and manifest.

Beachcombing is also an activity that is incredibly therapeutic and nothing beats wandering along the shores, lost in your thoughts, searching for that one perfectly imperfect piece of sea glass or battered bit of broken pottery. There is something really cathartic about it and you can then use these pieces of treasure to create masterpieces of art along the shore.

Creating a beach mandala from your beachcombing treasures can be done on your own or you can share the experience within a group and it doesn't need to take hours to do. It's totally up to you how long you spend. So, as you've gathered all your treasures together, and you've embraced the sounds of the waves, the birds and being "at one with nature, you can start to create your mandala. Always paying attention to the thoughts that come up and the stories that you create around the repetitive pattern of your art. You can ask yourself how do these thoughts reflect in your own life just now?

Then, when you're finished, you can watch as the rising tide washes it all away, or maybe the wind blows it across the beach. Reminding us that we are not permanent, nothing is and that what you're going through, will pass.

Most groups will gather after their swims for a chat over a hot tea and some cake, but I love the warmer nights for a cosey fire on the beach after swims. These really are the perfect times for warming up and get to know your fellow dippers. My first group swim was followed by a "blether" around the fire afterwards. This is where I was able to ask questions and listen to stories and really just soak up the full atmosphere of why dippers dip. It's magical, it's warming, it's welcoming and it's perfect on a Summer night toasting marshmallows and sipping hot chocolate. Times like this around the fire that really build your confidence and Self Esteem.

I remember realising at this point that we are all the same, nobody cares about how they look, everyone just wants to enjoy their "dook" and soon, you will be just the same.

These gatherings around the fire reminded me of an empowerment call I was co-hosting a few years ago. One of the women had shared a story about her own self-worth. She didn't feel she could justify spending money on a custom made item of clothing for herself, even though she knew it would be well worn. It was a beautiful story about how she overcame the guilt and shame of not feeling like she deserved to splash out on herself.

Well, on the same day as that call, Facebook had shown me a memory from 7 years before where I too had felt so guilty for buying something for myself.

A designer brand lipstick in fact. Now, thinking back to that day, I actually tried to justify the splurge of cash to myself in so many ways. I even tried to bargain with myself about how often I would wear it and when. It took me about 45 minutes to pick the colour because I wanted to make sure it was a colour that would be worn often. I really wanted the lipstick, but it was pricey and I nearly walked away 3 times without buying.

I didn't realise it at the time, but looking back now I can see the guilt was because I didn't think I deserved the high value item and I would feel like a fake every time I pulled it out of my make up bag to put it on. Making assumptions about what other people would think of me. It was as if I would have to torture myself every time I wore it to justify its value.

Shocking isn't it? But how does this relate to outdoor swimming and dipping? Well, it's simple and I hear stories like this all the time from dippers, mostly those new to it and before they have even set foot on the beach. Each one worried about what others will think of them because they don't have the right equipment or from those who are self-conscious about how they will look in their swim suit or in photos.

Here's the thing though, none of us who are already dipping actually care about what you wear of how you look. We too have been in your shoes, so we can totally relate to how you are feeling, but we swim because we want to swim, not because we want to look good for other people. With all these cold water groups, you will soon realise that it's not a fashion show out there. There is a funny phrase we often hear repeated within the community, "all dry robe and no knickers" because we forgo the underwear after dipping. It's just too difficult to put it back on when our skin is still damp. Think back to changing at the swimming pool as a child and quite literally getting your knickers in a twist.

Now imagine getting yourself in a twist in the middle of a carpark…it doesn't bare thinking about, does it. So, always swim for you and not for anyone else.

Your confidence will grow, the more you go. But to have these gorgeous stories as reminders to help you along the way will be invaluable on your journey and something I wish I had access to when I started dipping myself. Had I known how everyone else was feeling for their first time, I would have done it long ago.

Nonetheless, I started when I did and it all worked out just fine. As it will for you and soon enough you will be wandering around in your pyjamas, wearing a cosey pair of fluffy crocs, a dry robe and "no knickers". Not giving a hoot about anyone else's opinion of you.

## Miss Motivation

Just in case you need more encouragement, I asked on our swimming group The Fife Floaters, for our followers to give me one word that describes how Wild Swimming and Cold Water Therapy makes them feel, here's some of the words they gave me.;

Weightless. Amazing. Revitalised. Energised. Home. Free. Peace. Pain-free. Relaxed. Happy. Buzzing. Reset. Chilled. Spectacular. Smile. Content. Carefree. Childlike. Stress-free. Out of body. Inner child. Total Reset. Light. Mental Clarity. Cold. Brain Reset. Exhilarated. Stillness. Silence. Human. Thrilled. Relief. Grateful. Grounded. Uplifted. Elated. Electrifying. Charged. Indescribable. Mindfulness. Meditative. Belonging. Self Care. Self Love. Joy. Laughter. Friendships. Soulful. Alive. Community.

That's a pretty good list right there and if you're still in any doubt, trust me, it's alright once you're in.

# Health, Healing and Happiness

So, we already know that the cold water is great for our health and when we choose health and invest in exercise, nutrition, hydration our body produces the hormones we need to function properly and effectively. Our blood sugar levels are balanced and we have more energy, burning fat to help us either stay warm in the cold water or to support working muscles. All of which helps us sleep better which ties in nicely with our mental health because more sleep means clearer mind, freeing up space for joy and laughter and when we are happy, your body rewards you with an influx of serotonin, oxytocin, dopamine and endorphins. All these hormones are essential to a healthy heart, mind and digestion.

When you choose healing, you're choosing yourself. You recognise that you're important enough to deserve happiness and health. You're choosing to invest in yourself. You recognise your value, your self worth and how important it is, as a woman to be happy and healthy FOR YOU first.

So, ask yourself-

Do you BELIEVE you DESERVE BETTER?

Are you ready to challenge yourself beyond your negative thought patterns?

Are you ready to push through the boundaries of your comfort zone?

Are you ready to shift your mind-set from "I don't have

time" to "I am MAKING THE TIME".

Are you ready to make yourself a PRIORITY?

Allow this book to CHALLENGE you.

Allow this book to MOTIVATE you and ENCOURAGE you.

Allow this book to INSPIRE you and SUPPORT you.

Allow this book to help you HEAL both physically and mentally.

Allow this book to remind you that You are enough.

I hope you can see how incredible you are and who you can be if you just put your mind to it.

You are enough.

A bright shining star, beautiful, magnificent. Just as you are.

Just get out there and enjoy the freedom the ocean gives you. What are you waiting for? Stop complaining. Stop moaning. Stop wallowing in self pity. Stop pretending everything is OK. Stop telling yourself life is awful. Stop comparing yourself to other people. Stop comparing your home, your car, your job, your family, your bank balance. Stop pushing yourself too hard. Stop exhausting your mind, your body, your soul. Stop creating drama. Stop telling yourself you cant. Stop telling yourself no. Stop not trusting your instincts. Stop being lazy. Stop eating crap.

Stop putting things off. Just, STOP.

Start complementing yourself. Start rejoicing. Start enjoying self care. Start admitting when things aren't going right. Start telling yourself that life is amazing, because it really is. Start comparing yourself to your yester self. Start asking yourself "am I doing my best?". Start spending time with your family, in your home, out in your car, outdoors. Start resting when you're tired. Start going to bed earlier. Start getting up earlier. Start eating more fruit, more vegetables. Start drinking more water. Start walking. Start listening to your body. Start telling yourself anything is possible. Start listening to music. Start with a small thing. Start the ball rolling. Start caring about you instead of caring about what others think. Start now.

As soon as you start taking positive steps to change your negative pattern, the universe will present to you the right path if you just let go and trust that everything happens for a reason. Things fall apart, people change, life gives you challenges...they're all meant to be and they clear the path for what's coming.

Have faith that everything is just temporary and that the tough times pass, just as quickly as the good times come.

When you can, take chances, grab opportunities, push yourself to do bigger and better things. It's all part of the bigger plan and you don't want to miss out.

And all of a sudden...You will realise that in order for you to look after everyone else, your own health is more important.

You will realise you didn't need to do this on your own

anymore and you had the support of so many other women who all want the best for you.

You will realise it's OK to ask for help and that you aren't weak for doing so. Nobody will be judging you, but even if they are, they don't matter. What other people think of you is none of your business.

See your potential, and tap into it fully. See your worth and stop giving your power away.

Release your past. It's in the past and the longer you hold on to it, the longer it will hold you back from your future.

See how important it is for your health to nourish your body.

See how important it is for your mind to practice daily self care rituals.

See how important it is to cry. Tears are salt and salt heals wounds.

See that self care can be ugly, it can be messy and it can be rough. It's not just bubble baths and candles.

Know that your story isn't over, this is just the beginning. The beginning of a beautiful story, an incredible journey and the start of some amazing relationships.

See your worth and take a chance on yourself. You have nothing to lose and it has to work because how things were just now, isn't working.

Recognise that none of the above is selfish and all of it is necessary.

Say yes to yourself and start nit just a new chapter, but a whole different book.

You deserve to feel happy, good, taken care of and to not feel guilty for taking care of you own needs first.

Self Care is essential, not optional.

# Conscious Living

Below are some really good tips for living in an awareness of self and your surroundings. Ideal for the fast-paced world we live in today and perfect to incorporate into your everyday dipping.

1. Try not to get caught up in the details of what's going on around you. You will soon realise that you will have more time to enjoy life and life will be in flow.

2. Practice meditation and journaling. This helps you deep dive into your emotions so you can understand yourself, your reactions and your dreams, and fears. This awareness is so important in the fast paced competitive world we live in today..

3. Share your knowledge with others as often as you can and support each other in yours and theirs growth, building rapport and strong relationships.

4. Be careful with what you allow into your energy field. We are continually being bombarded with negative news, war, pain, poverty and hate, so be mindful about what you watch and who you listen to.

5. Although there is much ugliness in the world, there is also so much beauty too. Look for the beauty in every day and as often as you can.

6. If you are not already part of a circle/group/community nurture this. These groups and circles become good friends

and sometimes they become family too. Having these connections gives you a great source of caring companions which are your ties to your community.

7. Think outside the box and always look at the wider picture. Read often. Explore all your options. Travel, see the world. Widen your horizons.

8. Embrace the difficulties in life. They are there to teach you and everything you go through, whether good or bad is all part of your journey.

9. Dance to your own beat. Move around often. Movement is the best way to bring you back in to your own body. It allows you to feel again and moves out old energy. Movement connects us to the earth and grounds us.

10. Seek solitude. When the world is noisy, it can be so difficult to find peace and time to relax. Make a point of seeking out this solace.

# The Wild in the Waves

The Wild Wind Blows

While the wild wind blows strong today
I wonder what it carries away.
Maybe it will take my worries and woes
Or even my pain, I hope that goes.
Either way, I count my blessings
And allow myself, no longer obsessing.
To feel the breath of the wind and sea
As the cleansing waves wash over me
The waves, the wind, the sand below
Let them carry what needs to go

LjG

# Outdoor Swimming Groups

This list is merely a snapshot of the outdoor swimming community and I do apologise in advance that most of the ones listed are based in Scotland. As a Scottish dooker myself, I've joined loads of other Scottish groups. There are however, so many more based all over the world, including the one in Australia who we connect with often and a solo dooker in Canada. I'm sure that by finding some of these wonderful communities you will absolutely find some new friends along the way too.

Fife Floaters – Kirkcaldy, Scotland
Fife Dippers Mental Health Dipping Society – Leven, Scotland
The Swans of a Beach – Lower Largo, Scotland
Leven Looney Dookers Fife – Leven, Scotland
Wild Skins – East Neuk Fife, Scotland
Seafield Sinkers – Kirkcaldy, Scotland
The Bonnie Black Swans – Various Locations, Scotland
Dookin' Dragons – West Scotland
Cruix Dooks! – Lanarkshire, Scotland
The Ferry Dunkers – Broughty Ferry, Scotland
Pittenweem Menopausal Mermaids (swims) – Pittenweem Tidal Pool, Scotland
Nevis Dippers – North West Scotland
Salty Sisters Dunbar – East Lothian, Scotland
Wild Wimmin Swimmin – Venachar, Scotland
Longniddry Sea Swimmers – East Lothian, Scotland
West Lothian Dippers – Central Scotland
Paisley Wild Swimming Buddies – West Scotland
Strathearn Outdoor Swimmers – Loch Earn, Scotland
Warrior Water Women – Glasgow, Scotland

Polar Bear Club – Rivers around Scotland
Edinburgh Bluetits – Portobello, Edinburgh
Bluetoon Bay Buddies – Aberdeen, Scotland
Salty Bitches – Victoria, Australia
The Cold Water Therapist – Linlithgow, Scotland
The Water Wavers – Various Locations around Scotland
Aberdeen Aquaholics – Aberdeen, Scotland

Kinghorn Sea Swimmers – Fife, Scotland
Baywatch Burntisland – Fife, Scotland
Cold Water Exposure – Ayrshire, Scotland
Beyond the Blue – Dorset, England
Bath Open Water Beauts – Somerset, England
Chill Perthshire – Perthshire, Scotland
Coldingham Brave Bayers – Scottish Borders
Mad Piranhas – Prestwick, Scotland
Edinburgh Blue Balls – Joppa, Edinburgh, Scotland
Inchbaggers Loch Lomond Island swims – Scotland
The Dookers – South Lanarkshire, Scotland
White Loch Wild Water Women – E Renfrewshire, Scotland
Wild Swim – mighty mermaids Stonehaven, Scotland
Mental Health Swims – Silver Sands, Aberdour
Highland Otters – Inverness, Scotland
Eden Springs Wild Swimmers – Eden Springs Fishery
Willowgate Activity Centre – Perth, Scotland
Dundee Dookers – Broughty Ferry, Scotland
Linlithgow Selkies – West Lothian, Scotland
Swimmy Gimmy – Banff, Scotland
Duck Bay Dippers – Loch Lomond, Scotland
Cruden Bay Harbour Dookers – Aberdeenshire, Scotland
The Dell Dippers – Faskally Pitlochry, Scotland
Inverness Open Water Swimming – Inverness, Scotland
The Montrose Polar Bears – Angus, Scotland
The IceGuys – Tyneside, England

Dundee Selkies – Scotland
Wild Dookers – Keith, Scotland
Cairngorm Wild Swimmers – Highlands, Scotland
Barassie Sea Swimmers – Ayrshire, Scotland
Broch Selkies (Wild Dookers) – Moray, Scotland
Lochaber Loons – Fort William, Scotland
Selkies of the Clyde – Inverclyde, Scotland
Sink or Swim – Portobello, Edinburgh, Scotland

# References and Articles of interest

https://www.everydayhealth.com/wellness/cold-water-therapy/guide/#:~:text=How%20long%20should%20I%20stay,start%20to%20shake%20or%20shiver.

https://www.bupa.co.uk/newsroom/ourviews/cold-water-therapy

https://www.beachcombingmagazine.com/blogs/news/i-want-to-age-like-sea-glass

https://www.facebook.com/bernadette.noll

https://wyldemoon.co.uk/the-moon/phases-of-the-moon/

https://www.port.ac.uk/news-events-and-blogs/blogs/health-and-wellbeing/cold-water-therapy-what-are-the-benefits-and-dangers-of-ice-baths-wild-swimming-and-freezing-showers

https://www.sas.org.uk/take-action/fundraise-with-us/dip-a-day/dip-a-day-safety-guidance/

https://www.marieclaire.co.uk/life/health-fitness/cold-water-therapy-benefits-707395

https://www.bhf.org.uk/informationsupport/heart-matters-magazine/activity/cold-water-swimming

https://seasoulblessings.com/2020/07/22/five-simple-sea-rituals-to-transform-your-day/

https://rnli.org/

Printed in Great Britain
by Amazon